Touched by an E-mail
FOR
MOTHERS

Touched by an E-mail

FOR
MOTHERS

Bridge-Logos *Publishers*

North Brunswick, New Jersey 08902 USA

TOUCHED BY AN E-MAIL FOR MOTHERS
Edited by Denny Mog
Copyrightc1999 by Bridge-Logos Publishers
Library of Congress Catalog Card Number: 99-69698
International Standard Book Number: 0-88270-794-9

Published by:

Bridge-Logos *Publishers*
1300 Airport Road, Suite E
North Brunswick, NJ 08902
http://www.bridgelogos.com

Dedication:

To my Mom,
Lydabell

*She thought her name was funny,
so she called herself Jane*

INTRODUCTION

Dear Mom,

I never told you enough how much I loved you. Now that you're gone, I'm sorry about that. Of course, none of us ever tell those we love that we do love them quite enough during their lifetimes. Most of us think of it after it's too late. That's sad.

I loved the way you cared for Dad and for us kids, and when things got tough how you never complained and always had a good word for us. How you would always be on our side whether we were right or wrong. We must have broken your heart a number of times, but you never let on. I remember how you used to get up early, while we all still slept, so you could have the daily wash hanging on the line in the backyard. Oh, the wonderful smell of our clothes after drying in the morning sun!

I remember how excited you got about some things – like taking the grandkids to the park to feed the ducks. You could always come up with a bag of stale bread for the ducks. And I can see you talking to the radio when the Cincinnati Reds were losing a big game or some talk show host was spouting what you believed was "nonsense." Yes, you were opinionated, but you were usually right. It seemed like the older I got the "more right" you became. I remember being a small kid about five or six when the Reds won the pennant. You grabbed me by my arms and tossed me around the room. You were quite a fan! And I had quite a ride that day.

Mom, it's wonderful to think of you with such memories. Unfortunately, I know not everyone has been blessed with such a life's experience. There has to be a certain sadness in their lives. You loved to laugh, and you really loved to do things for people when they needed help. Even in your latter days, you were worrying about neighbors who needed this or that. I was always proud of you for being this way.

I'm sorry you're not here to read this book. Heck, you weren't even around long enough to even know what the Internet is, but I think you would have loved it. I remember receiving your wonderful, loving letters, and E-mail would have made it so much easier for you. And I know you would have loved the stories and poems in this volume – stories I've culled from my E-mail and from the Internet — because they would confirm for you something I know you believed — that most folks are good, caring people who like to have fun, who occasionally have problems they can overcome and who usually learn to survive, as you did, by persevering.

I hope the moms who do see this book will find some enjoyment, some peace, some inspiration in its pages. It's dedicated to you, but written for them.

Love,
Denny
December 1999

A Mother's Prayer

Dear Lord, it's such a hectic day,
With little time to stop and pray
For life's been anything but calm
Since you called me to be a mom.

Running errands, matching socks,
Building dreams with building blocks.
Cooking, cleaning, and finding shoes
And other stuff that children lose.

Fitting lids on bottles of bugs,
Wiping tears and giving hugs.
A stack of last week's mail to read,
So where's the quiet time I need?

Yet when I steal a minute, Lord
Just at the sink or ironing board

To ask the blessings of Your grace,
I see then in my small one's face
That You have blessed me all the while
And I stop to kiss that precious smile.

Handwriting on the Wall

A weary mother returned from the store, lugging large bags of groceries. Awaiting her arrival was her 8-year-old son, eager to tell what his young brother had done.

"While I was out playing and dad was on the telephone," he said, "T.J. took his crayons and wrote on the wall. It's on the new wallpaper you just hung in the den, and I told him you would be really angry.""

Mom let out a moan and furrowed her brow. "Where is your little brother right now," she asked. And she marched to his closet where he was hiding.

She called his full name as she entered his room. He trembled with fear. For the next ten minutes she ranted and raved about how he had ruined the expensive wallpaper. The more she scolded, the more angry she became.

She headed to the den to see the damage, and when she saw the wall her eyes flooded with tears. The message she read pierced her soul with a dart. It said, "I love Mommy," surrounded by a heart.

Well, the wallpaper remained just as she had found it with an empty frame around the heart. It was a constant reminder to her to read the handwriting on the wall.

13

No Threat

A man of quality is not threatened by a woman of equality.

If Tomorrow Never Comes

If I knew it would be the last time I'd see you fall asleep, I would tuck you in more tightly and pray the Lord, your soul to keep.

If I knew it would be the last time I'd see you walk out the door, I would give you a hug and kiss and call you back for one more.

If I knew it would be the last time I'd hear your voice lifted up in praise, I would video tape each action and word, so I could play them back day after day.

If I knew it would be the last time I could spare an extra minute or two to stop and say "I love you," instead of assuming, you would know I do.

If I knew it would be the last time I would be there to share your day, I'm sure I wouldn't just let this one slip away.

15

But surely, we often think there's always tomorrow to make up for an oversight, and we always get a second chance to make everything right.

We believe there will always be another day to say "I love you," and certainly another chance to ask, "Anything I can do?"

But just in case we might be wrong, and today is all we get, let's say how much "we love you," how much "we won't forget."

Tomorrow is not promised to anyone, young and old alike. And today may be the last chance to hold your loved one tight.

So if you're waiting for tomorrow, why not do it today? If tomorrow never comes, you'll surely regret the day that you didn't take the extra time for a smile, a hug or a kiss. That you said you were too busy to give someone what turns out to be their one last wish.

So hold your loved ones close today, whisper in their ear. Tell them how much you love them and that you'll always hold them dear. Take time to say "I'm sorry," "Please forgive me," "Thank you" or "It's okay."

And if tomorrow never comes, you'll not regret today."

He's Out There

Little Cory was afraid of the dark. One night his mother told him to go out to the back porch and bring her the broom.

The child turned to his mother and said, "Mama, I don't want to go out there. It's dark."

The mother smiled reassuringly at her son. "You don't have to be afraid of the dark," she explained. "Jesus is out there. He'll look after you and protect you."

The little boy looked at his mother real hard and asked, "Are you sure He's out there?"

"Yes, I'm sure. He is everywhere, and He is always ready to help you when you need Him," she said.

Corey thought about that for a minute and then went to the back door and cracked it open a tiny bit. Peering into the darkness, he called, "Jesus? If You're out there, would You please hand me the broom?"

Cheering Section

Everyone needs recognition for their accomplishments, but few people make the need known quite as clearly as little Jeremy, who said to his mother:

"Let's play darts. "I'll throw them and you say 'Wonderful!'"

I'm Going to Bed

A mother and dad were watching TV when the mother said, "I'm tired and it's getting late. I think I'll go to bed."

She went to the kitchen to make the sandwiches for the next day's lunches, rinsed out the popcorn bowls, took meat out of the freezer for supper the following evening, checked the cereal box levels, filled the sugar container, put spoons and bowls on the table, and readied the coffee pot for brewing the next morning.

She then put some wet clothes in the dryer, put a load of clothes into the wash, ironed a shirt and secured a loose button. She picked up the newspapers strewn on the floor, picked up the game pieces left on the table, and put the telephone book back into the drawer. She watered the plants, emptied a wastebasket and hung up a towel to dry.

She yawned and stretched and headed for the bedroom. She stopped by the desk and wrote a note to the teacher, counted out some cash for the field trip, and pulled a textbook out from hiding under a chair. She signed a birthday card for a friend, addressed and stamped the envelope, and wrote a quick note for the grocery store. She put both near her purse. She then cleaned her face, put on moisturizer, brushed and flossed her teeth and trimmed her nails.

Dad called and said, "I thought you were going to bed."

"I'm on my way," she said. She put some water into the dog's dish, put the cat outside, then made sure the doors were locked. She looked in on each of the kids and turned out a bedside lamp, hung up a shirt, threw some dirty socks in the hamper, and had a brief conversation with one child still up doing homework.

In her own room, she set the alarm, laid out clothing for the next day, and straightened up the shoe rack.

She added three things to her list of things to do tomorrow.

About that time, the dad turned off the TV and announced to no one in particular, "I'm going to bed." And he did.

Seven Gifts to Give Today

The Gift of Really Listening
But you must really listen.
No interrupting, no daydreaming
No planning your response.
Just listening.

The Gift of Affection
Be generous with appropriate hugs,
Kisses, pats on the back and handholds.
Let these small actions demonstrate
The love you have for family and friends.

The Gift of Laughter
Clip a cartoon, tell a joke, share a funny story.
Your gift will say, "I love to laugh with you."

The Gift of a Written Note
It can be a simple "thank you" or a complete letter.

A brief note can make someone's day,
Or it may even change their life.

The Gift of a Compliment
A simple and sincere, "you look great."
Telling someone "great job!" or
"That was a wonderful effort,"
Will bring joy to anyone's heart.

The Gift of Doing a Favor
Every day, go out of your way
To do something kind for someone else.

The Gift of Cheerfulness
The easiest way to feel good is
To make someone else feel good.
It is easy to do. Just smile and say,
"Hello, have a great day!"

A Child's Angel

Once upon a time, a child was about to be born. So she asked God, "How am I going to live there on earth? I'll be so small and helpless."

And God answered, "Among the many angels, I chose one for you. She will be waiting for you and take care of you."

The child then said, "Here in heaven I don't do anything but sing and smile. That's enough for me to be happy."

God answered, "Your angel will sing for you and will also smile for you every day. And you will feel your angel's love and be happy.

The child asked, "How will I learn?" I don't know the language that men talk."

God said, "Your angel will tell you the most beautiful and sweet words you will ever hear, and with patience and care your angel will teach you how to live."

The child asked, "What am I going to do when I want to talk to you?"

God smiled, "Your angel will place your hands together and will teach you how to pray."

The child pleaded, "Who will protect me?"

God said, "Your angel will defend you even if it means risking its life."

At that moment there was much peace in heaven, but voices from earth could already be heard, and the child in a hurry asked softly, "Oh, God, if I am about to leave now, please tell me my angel's name."

"Your angel's name is of no importance," God said, 'but you will call her 'mommy.'"

I'm Going to Celebrate

This morning when I awoke I suddenly realized that this is the best day of my life! There were times yesterday when I wondered if I would make it to today; but I did! And because I did, I'm going to celebrate.

Today, I'm going to celebrate what an unbelievable life I have had: the accomplishments, the many blessings, and even the hardships because they have served to make me stronger.

I will go through today with my head held high and with a happy heart. I will marvel at God's seemingly simple gifts: the morning dew, the sun, the clouds, the trees, the flowers and the birds.

Today, I will share my excitement for life with others. I'll make someone smile. I'll perform an act of kindness for someone I don't even know. Today, I'll compliment someone who seems down. I'll tell a child how special they are, and I'll tell someone I love just how dear they are to me.

Today is the day I quit worrying about what I don't have and start being grateful for all the wonderful things God has already given me. I'll remember that to worry is just a waste of time because of my faith in God and His Divine Plan.

Tonight before I go to bed, I'll go outside and raise my eyes to the heavens. I will stand in awe of His creation, and I will praise God for these magnificent treasures.

As the day ends and I lay down to sleep, I will thank the Lord for the best day of my life. And I will go to sleep, excited with expectation because I know tomorrow is going to be even better than today!

No Time

I knelt to pray but not for long,
I had too much to do.
I had to hurry and get to work
For bills would soon be due.

So I knelt and said a hurried prayer,
And jumped up off my knees.
My Christian duty was now done
My soul could rest at ease.

All day long I had no time
To spread a word of cheer.
No time to speak of Christ to friends,
They'd laugh at me I fear.

No time, no time, too much to do,
That was my constant cry,

No time to give to souls in need,
But at last the time, the time to die.

I went before the Lord,
I came, I stood with downcast eyes.
For in His hands God held a book;
It was the book of life.

God looked into His book and said
"Your name I cannot find.
I once was going to write it down,
But never found the time.

I Love You

The greatest weakness of most humans is their
hesitancy to tell others how much they love them
while they're still alive.

Faith is Knowing

When you come to the end of all the light you know,
and you are about to step off into the darkness of the
unknown, faith is knowing one of two things
will happen.

There will be something solid to stand on,
or you will be taught to fly.

The Little One is for Me

A chaplain was visiting a delightful elderly lady in the hospital. As he approached her bed, he noticed that with the index finger of one hand she was touching, one by one, the fingers of the other. She had her eyes closed.

When the chaplain spoke to her, she opened her eyes and said, "Ah, pastor, I was just saying my prayers – the prayers my mother taught me many years ago."

The chaplain looked puzzled, so the lady went on to explain. "I hold my hand like this with my thumb towards me. That reminds me to pray for those nearest me. Then, there is my pointing finger, so I pray for those who point the way to others, like teachers, leaders and parents. The next finger is the biggest, so I pray for those in high places. After that comes the weakest finger – look it won't stand up by itself, so I pray for the sick and the lonely and the afraid.

"And this little one – well, last of all I pray for myself."

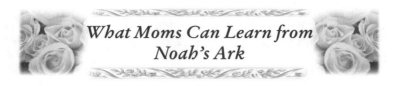

What Moms Can Learn from Noah's Ark

1. Plan ahead. It wasn't raining when Noah built the ark.
2. Stay fit. When you're 600 years old, someone might ask you to do something really big.
3. Don't listen to critics. Do what has to be done.
4. Take care of your animals as if they were the last ones on earth.
5. Stay below deck in a storm.
6. When the doo-doo gets really deep, don't sit there and complain – shovel!
7. Remember that the ark was built by amateurs, and the Titanic was built by professionals.
8. Remember that the woodpeckers inside are often a bigger threat than the storm outside.
9. No matter how bleak it looks, there's always a rainbow on the other side.
10. Don't miss the boat.

To Be Loved

Woman was created from the rib of man;
Not from his head to be thought of only,
Nor from his hand to be owned,
Nor from his foot to be beneath,
But from under his arm to be protected,
From his side to be equal,
And from his heart to be loved.

A Plan that Works

A married couple were celebrating their 60th wedding anniversary. At the party everyone wanted to know how they managed to stay married for so long — particularly in this day and age.

The husband responded. "When we were first married, we came to an agreement. I would make all the major decisions and my wife would make all the minor decisions. And in 60 years of marriage, we have never needed to make a major decision."

Take a Break, Mom

Take a break, Mom, and sit by the river. Watch the current quietly flow. Think for a moment, Mom, about where the current is going, the shores it will brush on its way, the clouds reflected on its surface, the animals that will come to drink from it, the leaves it gently nudges downstream.

Our lives sometimes seem like the river, wandering to the west, the south, back toward the east, seemingly without direction. And yet, Mom, we can take comfort in this thought, for like the river, we are always headed in the direction we are meant to go. Without trying, Mom, without knowing, we are part of the larger pattern of things, and we nourish many others just by passing through their lives.

Hugs

There's something in a simple hug
That always warms the heart;
It welcomes us back home,
And makes it easier to part.

A hug's a way to share the joy
And sad times we go through,
Or just a way for friends to say
They like you 'cause you're you.

Hugs are meant for anyone
For whom we really care,
From your grandma to your neighbor,
Or a cuddly teddy bear.

A hug is an amazing thing.
It's just the perfect way

To show the love we're feeling
But can't find the words to say.

It's funny how a little hug
Makes everyone feel good;
In every place and language,
It's always understood.

And hugs don't need new equipment,
Special batteries or parts.
Just open up your arms
And open up your hearts.

I'm Painting Now the Picture

When my hair is thin and silvered,
and my time of toil is through;
When I've many years behind me,
and ahead of me a few;
I shall want to sit, I reckon,
sort of dreaming in the sun;
And recall the roads I've traveled
and the many things I've done.

I hope there will be no picture
that I'll hate to look upon;
When the time to paint it better
or to wipe it out is gone.
I hope they will be no vision
of a hasty word I've said
That has left a trail of sorrow,
like a whip welt sore and red.
And I hope my old age dreaming

will bring back no bitter scene
Of a time when I was selfish,
of a time when I was mean.

When I'm getting old and feeble,
and I'm far along life's way,
I don't want to sit regretting
any bygone yesterday.

I am painting now the picture
that I'll want someday to see;
I am filling in a canvas
that will soon come back to me.
Though nothing great is on it,
and though nothing there is fine,
I shall want to look it over
when I'm old, and call it mine.

So I do not dare to leave it
while the paint is warm and wet,
With a single thing upon it
that I later will regret.

Worry

Worry does not empty tomorrow of its sorrow;
it empties today of its strength.

Home Efficiency

A husband recently attended a class on efficiency in the workplace.

The instructor concluded his lecture with a warning, "You probably don't want to try these techniques at home."

"Why not?" the husband asked.

"Well," the instructor explained, "I watched my wife's routine at breakfast for years. She made numerous trips to the refrigerator, stove, table and cabinets, often carrying just a single item at a time. That's when I suggested, 'Honey, why don't you try carrying several things at once?'"

The husband asked, "Did it save time?"

The instructor replied, "Actually, yes. It used to take her 20 minutes to get breakfast ready. Now I do it in seven."

Say, "Cheese"

Little Marianne walked daily to and from school. Though the weather this particular morning was questionable and clouds were forming, she made her trek to the elementary school. As the afternoon progressed, the winds whipped up, along with thunder and lightening.

The child's mother, concerned that her daughter would be frightened and possibly harmed by the storm, got into her car and drove along the route to the school.

As she did so, she saw her daughter walking along happily. But at each flash of lightning the child would stop, look up, and smile.

Stopping the car, the mother called to the child to get in with her. As they drove home, the girl continued to turn toward each lightning flash and smile.

The mother asked, "Marianne, what are you doing?"

The child answered, "Well, I have to keep smiling. God keeps taking pictures of me."

Encouragement

A number of frogs were traveling through the woods. Two of them fell into a deep pit. All the other frogs gathered around the pit, When they saw how deep the pit was, they told the two frogs they were as good as dead.

The two frogs ignored their comments and tried with all of their strength to jump out of the pit. The other frogs kept telling them to stop, that they were as good as dead.

Finally, one of the two frogs took heed what the other frogs were saying. He gave up, fell down and died.

The other frog continued to jump as hard as he could. Once again, the other frogs yelled at him to stop the pain and just die. He jumped even harder and finally made it out of the pit.

When he got out, the other frogs asked him, "Didn't you hear us?" The frog explained to them that he was deaf. All along, he thought they were encouraging him!"

Growing

The most beautiful discovery that true friends can make is that they can grow separately without growing apart.

It's The Thought That Counts

Three sons left home, went out on their own and prospered. Getting back together, they talked about the gifts they were able to give their elderly mother.

The first son said, "I built Mom a big house." The second said, "I sent her a big, new automobile with a driver." The third son smiled and said, "I've got you both beat. You remember how Mom enjoyed reading the Bible? And you know now she can't see very well. So I sent her a remarkable parrot that recites the entire Bible. It took elders in the church 12 years to teach him. He's one of a kind. Mama just has to name the chapter and verse, and the parrot recites it."

Soon thereafter, Mom sent out her letters of thanks:

"Matthew," she wrote one son, "The house you built is so huge. I live in only one room, but I have to clean the whole place."

"Duane," she wrote the second son, "I am too old to travel. I stay home most of the time, so I rarely use the automobile."

"Dearest Milton," she wrote the third son, "You have the good sense to know what your mother likes. The chicken was delicious."

I Am Thankful For . . .

1. The mess to clean after a party because it means I have been surrounded by friends.
2. The taxes I pay because it means I am employed.
3. The lady behind me in church who sings off key because it means that I can hear.
4. The piles of laundry and ironing because it means my loved ones are nearby.
5. The clothes that fit a little too snug because it means I have enough to eat.
6. A lawn that needs mowing, windows that need washing and gutters that need cleaning because it means I have a home.
7. The spot I find at the far end of the parking lot because it means I am capable of walking.
8. The alarm that goes off in the morning because it means I am alive.

A Special Place

There is a special place in life,
That needs my humble skill,
A certain job I'm meant to do,
Which no one else can fulfill.

The time will be demanding,
And the pay is not too good,
And yet, I wouldn't change it,
For a moment – if I could.

There is a special place in life,
A goal I must attain,
A dream that I must follow,
Because I won't be back again.

There is a mark that I must leave,
However small it seems to be,

A legacy of love for those
Who follow after me.

There is a special place in life,
That only I may share,
A little path that bears my name,
Awaiting me somewhere.

There is a hand that I must hold,
A word that I must say,
A smile that I must give,
For there are tears to blow away.

There is a special place in life,
That I was meant to fill.
A sunny spot where flowers grow,
Upon a windy hill.

There's always a tomorrow
And the best is yet to be,
And somewhere in this world,
I know there is a place for me.

A Little Misunderstanding

A mother sits at the airport anxiously awaiting her daughter's plane. The young lady is just returning from a far-away land where she had gone trying to find adventure.

As the daughter exits the plane, the mother notices a man directly behind her daughter. He is dressed in feathers with exotic markings all over his body, and he is carrying a shrunken head. The daughter introduces the man as her new husband.

The mother gasps in disbelief and disappointment and screams, "I said for you to marry a *rich* doctor! A *rich* doctor!"

Satan's Beatitudes

If the devil were to write his beatitudes, they would possibly go something like this:

Blessed are those who are too tired, too busy, too distracted to spend an hour a week in church. They are my best workers.

Blessed are those Christians who wait to be asked and expect to be thanked. I can use them.

Blessed are the touchy for with a bit of luck they may stop going to church. They are my missionaries.

Blessed are those who are very religious but get on everyone's nerves. They are mine forever.

Blessed are the troublemakers. They shall be called my children.

Blessed are those who have no time to pray. They are easy prey for me.

Blessed are the complainers. I'm all ears for them.

Blessed are you when you read this and think it is about other people. I've got you!

A Gift of Ears

"Can I see my baby?" the happy new mother asked. When the bundle was nestled in her arms and she moved the fold of cloth to look at his tiny face, she gasped. The baby had been born without ears.

As time passed, the mother learned that the baby's hearing was perfect. It was only his appearance that was marred.

After a few years, the boy rushed home from school one day and flung himself into his mother's arms. "A boy . . . a big boy . . . called me a freak," he cried. The mother sighed, knowing that his life was to be a series of heartbreaks.

He did reasonably well in school, developed some musical talents and had a number of friends. But he was never really comfortable with other people.

One day the boy's father learned that it was then possible to graft on a pair of outer ears, if they could be obtained. Thus, began the search for a person who would make such a sacrifice. Two years went by.

Finally, the father announced, "Son, you are going to the hospital. Your mother and I have found someone who will donate the ears you need. But it's a secret who it is."

The operation was a brilliant success, and a new person emerged. He became quite successful in life, but he always insisted, "Dad, I must know who gave so much for me. I could never do enough for him."

But the father would not tell. "The agreement was that you are not to know . . . not yet," he said.

The years kept their secret, but the day did come . . . one of the darkest days that ever pass by a son. He stood with his father over his mother's casket. Slowly, tenderly, the father stretched out his hand and raised her thick, reddish brown hair to reveal . . . his mother had no ears.

"Mother said she was glad she never let her hair be cut," the father whispered gently, "and nobody ever thought mother less beautiful, did they?"

Real love lies not is what is done and known, but in what is done and not known.

Confused Child

A certain little girl, when asked her name, would reply, "I'm Mr. Sugarbrown's daughter."

Her mother always corrected her. "You must say, 'I'm Jane Sugarbrown,'" the mother explained.

The following Sunday, the minister spoke to her in Sunday school and said, "Aren't you Mr. Sugarbrown's daughter?"

The little girl replied, "I thought I was, but mother says I'm not."

Smiling

Smiling is infectious; you can catch it like the flu,

When someone smiled at me today I started
smiling, too.

I passed around the corner there and someone saw
my grin

And when he smiled I realized I'd passed it on to him.

I thought about the smile and realized its worth,

A single smile like mine could travel round the earth.

So if you feel a smile begin don't leave it undetected.

Let's start an epidemic quick, and get the
world infected.

This Is What I've Learned

I've learned that a kindness done is never lost. It may take awhile. But like a suitcase on a luggage carousel, it will return again.

I've learned that just one person saying to me "You've made my day," makes my day.

I've learned that I feel better about myself when I make others feel better about themselves.

I've learned that being kind is more important than being right.

I've learned that one sincere apology is worth more than all the roses money can buy.

I've learned that the Lord didn't do it all in one day. What makes me think I can?

I've learned that I can't choose how I feel, but I can choose what I do about it.

I've learned that no matter how serious your life requires you to be, everyone needs a friend to act goofy with.

I've learned that no matter what their ages or how far away they may be, you never stop wanting to keep a protective arm around your children.

Best Friends

A woman and her dog were walking along a road enjoying the scenery when suddenly it occurred to her that she was dead. She remembered dying and that her dog had been dead for years. She wondered where the road was leading them.

After a while, they came to a high white stone wall along one side of the road. It looked like fine marble. As they walked along the wall, she saw a magnificent gate in a tall arch that looked like mother of pearl. The street that led to the gate looked like pure gold. Standing before the gate, she saw a man sitting at a desk to one side. "Excuse me, where are we?" she called out.

"This is heaven," the man answered.

"Wow," she said, "would you happen to have some water?"

"Of course, come right in, and I'll have some ice water brought right up." The man gestured, and the gate began to open.

"Can my friend," pointing at the dog, "come in, too?" the woman asked.

"I'm sorry, madam, but we don't accept pets," the man answered.

The woman thought a moment and then turned back toward the road and continued the way she had been going.

After another long walk, she came to a dirt road that led through a farm gate that looked as if it had never been closed. There was no fence. As she approached, she saw a young man leaning against a tree and reading a book.

"Excuse me," she called the reader. "Do you have any water?"

"Yeah, sure, there's a pump over there," he said. "Come on in."

"How about my friend here?" the woman asked.

"Sure," the young man answered, "there should be a bowl by the pump."

They went through the gate and sure enough there was an old-fashioned hand pump with a bowl beside it. The woman filled the bowl and took a long drink. Then she gave some to the dog. When they were full, the woman and her dog walked back toward the man at the gate.

"What do you call this place?" she asked.

"This is heaven," was the answer.

"Well, that's confusing," the woman replied. "The man down the road said that was heaven, too."

"Oh, you mean the place with the gold street and pearly gates? Nope, that's hell," the gatekeeper said.

"Doesn't it make you angry for them to use your name like that?" the woman asked.

"No. I can see how you might think so, but we're just happy that they screen out the folks who'll leave their best friends behind."

Kids Talk to God

Dear God:

- Is it true my father won't get in heaven if he uses bowling words in the house?

- What does it mean You are a jealous God? I thought You had everything!

- Did You really mean do unto others as they do unto You because if you did then I'm really going to get my brother?

- Maybe Cain and Abel would not kill each other so much if they had their own rooms. It works with my brother!

- I didn't think orange went with purple until I saw the sunset You made on Tuesday.

Natural Highs

- Laughing so hard your face hurts

- Lying in bed listening to the rain outside

- Finding a $20 bill in your coat from last winter

- Waking up to the smell of hot coffee that someone else has made for you

- Finding the sweater you want is on sale for half-price

- Riding a bike downhill

- Hot towels out of the dryer

- Seeing smiles and hearing laughter from your friends

- Mom telling you she loves you no matter how old you are

- Watching the expression on someone's face as they open a much-desired present from you

- Getting out of bed every morning and thanking God for another beautiful day

Little Thoughts to Think About

- May you have enough happiness to make you sweet, enough trials to make you strong, enough sorrow to keep you human, enough hope to make you happy, and enough money to buy gifts!

- When one door of happiness closes, another opens, but often we look so long at the closed door that we don't see the one that has opened.

- The best kind of friend is the one you could sit with on a porch swing, never saying a word, and then walk away feeling like that was the best conversation you ever had.

- Love starts with a smile, develops with a kiss and ends with a tear.

- Never say goodbye when you still want to try.

- The happiest of people don't necessarily have the best of everything; they just make the most of everything that comes their way.

- It's true that we don't know what we've got until we lose it, but it's also true that we don't know what we've been missing until it arrives.

- When you were born, you were crying and everyone around you was smiling. Live your life so that when you die, you're smiling and everyone around you is crying.

Words

A careless word may kindle strife;
A cruel word may wreck a life;
A timely word can level stress;
A loving word may heal and bless.

As Good As New

Don't be discouraged if your children reject your advice.

Years later they will offer it to their own offspring.

Scripture Scramble

There's this small general store that sits on the edge of a small town in Central Ohio. The owner is an elderly man who has attended church all his life. And like many general stores, this one always has two or three older gentlemen sitting around talking about how things "used to be."

The store owner has a habit of quoting Scripture every time he makes a transaction. And it's always a different verse. The old men now listen carefully every time a customer enters the store. They just want to know what the next verse will be.

One day not long ago, a Texan came in the store and inquired about a rug that was hanging on the wall. The man asked about the price of the rug, and the shop owner told him $400. But the owner and the old men all knew that the true worth was about $200.

So the Texan thought it over and finally said, I'll take it." He bought the rug and left the store.

The old men stared at the owner in anticipation of what possible Scripture could follow such a dishonest act. It was then that the owner said, "He was a stranger, and I took him in."

To The Women

Several years ago, a gathering of Native American men developed what they call the Seven Philosophies for a Native American man. They are intended to help guide Indian men on their journey through life. The first philosophy is called

"To the Women." It follows:

The cycle of life for the woman is the baby, girl, woman, and grandmother. These are the four directions of life.

She has been given by natural laws the ability to reproduce life. The most sacred of all things is life.

Therefore, all men should treat her with dignity and respect. Never was it our way to harm her mentally or physically. Indian men were never abusers. We always treated our women with respect and understanding. So from now on:

I will treat women in a sacred manner. The Creator gave women the responsibility for bringing new life into the world. Life is sacred, so I will look upon women in a sacred manner.

In our traditional ways, the woman is the foundation of the family. I will work with her to create a home atmosphere of respect, security and harmony. I will refrain from any form of emotional or physical abuse. If I have these feelings, I will talk to the Creator for guidance.

I will treat all women as if they were my own female relatives. This is my vow.

Good For The Soul

A mother took her children to a restaurant as a treat. Her six-year-old son asked if he could say grace.

As the family bowed their heads, the boy said, "God is good. God is great. Thank You for the food, and I would thank You even more if Mom gets us ice cream for dessert. And liberty and justice for all! Amen!"

Along with laughter from other customers nearby, a woman remarked, "That's what's wrong with this country. Kids today don't even know how to pray. Asking God for ice cream! Why, I never!

Hearing this, the small boy burst into tears and asked, "Did I do it wrong? Is God mad at me?"

His Mom held him and assured him that he had done a terrific job and God certainly was not mad at him.

And then an elderly gentlemen approached the table. He winked at the boy and said, "I happen to know that God thought that was a great prayer."

"Really," the boy asked.

"Cross my heart," the man said. Then the gentleman whispered as he pointed at the woman who made the remark, "Too bad she never asks God for ice cream. A little ice cream is good for the soul, sometimes."

Naturally, the family had their ice cream at the end of the meal. The young boy stared at his for a while and then did the unexpected. He picked up his sundae and without a word walked over and placed it in front of the woman.

With a big smile he told her, "Here, this is for you. Ice cream is good for the soul sometimes, and my soul is already good."

The Importance of One

One song can spark a moment

One flower can wake the dream

One tree can start a forest

One bird can herald spring

One smile begins a friendship

One handclasp lifts the soul

One star can guide a ship at sea

One word can frame the goal

One vote can change a nation

One sunbeam lights a room

One candle wipes out darkness

One laugh will conquer gloom

One step must start each journey

One word must start a prayer

One hope will raise our spirits

One touch can show you care

One voice can speak with wisdom

One heart can know what's true

One life can make a difference

By the Letters

Although things are not perfect
Because of trial or pain
Continue in thanksgiving
Do not begin to blame
Even when the times are hard
Fierce winds are bound to blow
God is forever able
Hold on to what you know
Imagine life without His love
Joy would cease to be
Keep thanking Him for all the things
Love imparts to thee
Move out of "Camp Complaining"
No weapon that is known
On earth can yield the power
Praise can do alone
Quit looking at the future
Redeem the time at hand

Start every day with worship
To "thank" is a command
Until we see Him coming
Victorious in the sky
We'll run the race with gratitude
EXalting God most high
Yes there will be good times and yes there will be bad, but
Zion waits in glory where none are ever sad!

No Load Too Heavy

A little boy was helping his dad move some books out of the attic into a larger room downstairs. It was important to this young boy that he was helping, even though he was probably getting in the way and slowing things down.

But the boy had a wise and patient father who knew it was more important to work at a task with his son than it was to move a pile of books efficiently. Among the books, however, were some rather large study books, and it was a chore for the boy to get them down the stairs.

On one particular trip, the boy dropped his pile of books several times. Finally, he sat down on the stairs and cried in frustration. He wasn't doing any good at all. He wasn't strong enough to carry the heavy books down the narrow stairway. It hurt him to think he couldn't do this for his daddy.

Without a word, however, the father picked up the dropped load of books, put them into the boy's arms, and scooped up both the boy and the books and carried them down the stairs.

And so they continued for load after load, both enjoying each other's company very much – the boy carrying the books and the dad carrying the boy.

Is God Showing Through?

A little girl, Meredith, on her way home from church, turned to her mother and said, "Mommy, the preacher's sermon this morning confused me."

The mother said, "Oh! Why is that?"

Meredith replied, "Well, he said that God is bigger than we are. Is that true?"

"Yes, that's true," the mother said.

"He also said God lives within us. Is that true, too?" the little girl asked.

Again the mother replied, "Yes."

"Well," said the girl, "If God is bigger than us and He lives in us, wouldn't He show through?"

Collect the Feathers

A woman repeated a bit of gossip about a neighbor. Within a few days the whole town knew the story. And the person it concerned was deeply hurt and offended.

Later, the woman responsible for spreading the rumor learned that it was completely untrue. She was very sorry and went to a wise old sage to find out what she could do to repair the damage.

"Go to the market," he said, "and purchase a chicken and have it killed. Then on your way home, pluck its feathers and drop them one by one along the road."

Although surprised by this advice, the woman did as she was told.

The next day, the wise man said, "Now go and collect

all those feathers you dropped yesterday and bring them back to me."

The woman followed the same road, but to her dismay the wind had blown all the feathers away. After searching for hours, she returned with only three in her hand.

"You see," said the old sage, "it's easy to drop them, but it's impossible to get them back. So it is with gossip. It doesn't take much to spread a rumor, but once you do, you can never completely undo the wrong."

Out of the Mouths of Babes . . .

As they were on the way to church services, a Sunday school teacher asked her class why it was important to be quiet in church.

One bright little girl named Rachel replied, "Because people are sleeping."

A Real Friend

A simple friend has never seen you cry.
A real friend has shoulders soggy from your tears.

A simple friend doesn't know your parents' first
names.
A real friend has their phone number in her address
book.

A simple friend brings a six-pack of soda to your
party.
A real friend comes early to help you cook and stays
late to help you clean.

A simple friend hates it when you call after she has
gone to bed.
A real friend asks you why it took so long to call.

A simple friend seeks to talk with you about your problems.
A real friend seeks to help you with your problems.

A simple friend, when visiting, acts like a guest.
A real friend opens your refrigerator and helps herself.

A simple friend thinks the friendship is over when you have an argument.
A real friend knows that it's not a friendship until after you've had a fight.

A simple friend expects you to always be there for them.
A real friend expects to always be there for you.

A Meadowlark Sang

A child whispered, "God, speak to me."
And a meadowlark sang.
The child did not hear.

So the child yelled, "God, speak to me."
And the thunder rolled across the sky.
But the child did not listen.

The child looked around and said, "God, let me see you."
And a star shone brightly.
But the child did not notice.

And the child shouted, "God, show me a miracle."
And a life was born.
But the child did not know.

So the child cried out in despair, "Touch me, God,
and let me know you're here."
Whereupon God reached down,
And touched the child.

But the child brushed away the butterfly,
And walked away without knowing.

Never Lose Hope

Hope is the rope that swings you through life.

Too Rough

Little Sue asked her mother, "Can I go outside and play with the boys?'

Her mother replied, "No, you can't play with the boys. They're too rough."

The small girl thought about it for a few moments and then asked, "If I can find a smooth one, can I play with him?"

The Interview

"Come in," God said to me. "So, you would like to interview Me?"

"If You have the time," I said.

God smiled and said, "My time is called eternity and is enough to do everything. What questions do you have to ask Me?"

"None that are new to You. What's the one thing that surprises You most about mankind?"

God answered: "That they get bored being children, are in a rush to grow up, and then long to be children again. That they lose their health to make money and then lose their money to restore their health. That by thinking anxiously about the future, they forget the present, so they live neither for the present nor the future. That they live as if they will never die, and they die as if they had never lived."

God took my hands, and we were silent.

After a long period, I said, "May I ask You another question? As a parent, what would You ask Your children to do?"

God replied with a smile:

"To learn that they cannot make anyone love them. To learn that it takes years to build trust, and a few seconds to destroy it.

"To learn that what is most valuable is not what they have in their lives, but who they have in their lives.

"To learn that it is not good to compare themselves to others. There will be others better or worse than they are.

"To learn that a rich person is not one who has the most, but is one who needs the least.

"To learn that they should control their attitudes, otherwise their attitudes will control them.

"To learn that it only takes a few seconds to open profound wounds in persons we love, and that it takes many years to heal them.

"To learn to forgive by practicing forgiveness.

"To learn that there are persons who love them dearly, but simply do not know how to show their feelings.

"To learn that true friends are scarce.

"To learn that it is not always enough that they be forgiven by others but that they forgive themselves.

"To learn that true happiness is not to achieve their goals but to learn to be satisfied with what they have already achieved.

"To learn that happiness is a decision.

"To learn that two people can look at the same thing and see something totally different.

"To learn that by trying to hold on to loved ones, they very quickly push them away; and by letting go of those they love, they will be by their side forever.

"To learn that they can never do anything to make Me love them. I simply do.

"To learn that the shortest distance they can be from Me is the distance of a prayer."

Things To Never Forget

Don't judge people by their relatives.

Never laugh at anyone's dreams.

Be the first to forgive.

Spend some time alone.

Read between the lines.

Never risk what you can't afford to lose.

What's right isn't always popular.

Your attitude is what people notice first.

Silence is sometimes the best answer.

Don't confuse kindness with weakness.

Do the right thing, regardless of what others think.

Judge people from where they stand.

The more you know, the less you fear.

Kindness

Kindness is never a waste.
If it has no effect on the recipient,
at least it benefits the bestower.

Kindness pays the most
when you don't do it for pay.

Kindness adds and multiplies
as we divide it with others.

It is when we forget ourselves that
we do things most likely to be
remembered.

I Asked God

I asked God for strength,
that I might achieve,
I was made weak
to humbly obey.

I asked God for health,
that I might do greater things,
I was given infirmity
that I might do better things.

I asked God for riches,
that I might be happy,
I was given poverty
that I might be wise.

I asked God for power,
that I might have the praise of me,
I was given weakness
that I might feel the need of God.

I asked God for all things,
that I might enjoy life,
I was given life
that I might enjoy all things.

I got nothing that I asked for,
but everything I had hoped for.
Almost despite myself
my unspoken prayers were answered.

I am among all women
most richly blessed.

The Life Of A Man

There are four stages to man:
when he believes in Santa Claus,
when he does not believe in Santa Claus,
when he is Santa Claus,
and when he looks like Santa Claus.

There But For The Grace Of God

It was a cold winter Sunday. The parking lot to the church was filling with cars. As folks left their cars, they noticed a tattered-looking man leaning against the wall of the church.

The man was almost lying down as if asleep. He wore a long trench coat that was almost in shreds. His toes were sticking out of holes in his shoes. And a hat topped his head, pulled down so far you couldn't see his face. As people walked quickly by into the church, they gossiped about the man, but no one invited him inside. Everyone assumed he was homeless.

A few moments later, as church was beginning, the congregation noticed that their pastor was not yet standing at the pulpit as he usually did. Then the doors to the church opened and the homeless man walked in. People stared at him and snickered as he walked down the aisle toward the front of the church. He stood behind the pulpit and took of his hat and coat.

It was then that everyone realized this was their pastor. He was the "homeless" man. No one said a word.

The pastor picked up his Bible and laid it on the pulpit and said, "Folks, I don't think I have to tell you what I'm preaching about today."

111

He Ought To Know

Three-year-old Matthew decided he could put his shoes on by himself.

His mother noticed the left shoe was on her son's right foot and the right shoe was on his left foot.

"Matthew," she said, "your shoes are on the wrong feet."

He looked at her with a raised brow and said, "Mom, you can't kid me! These are my feet."

The Picture On The Wall

There was a frantic knock at the doctor's office door.
It was a knock more urgent than he had ever heard
before. "Come in, come in," the doctor said as he
answered the knock.

In walked a frightened little girl, a child no more than
nine. "Oh, doctor, I beg you, please come with me.
My mother is dying, she is sick as she can be."

"I don't make house calls," the doctor answered,
"bring your mother here."

"But she's too sick," the girl replied. The doctor,
touched by her devotion, decided he would go.

The girl led him to her house, where her mother lay
in bed, The woman was so sick she could hardly raise
her head. But her eyes cried out for help and help her

the doctor did. The doctor got her fever down and by morning it was clear that the mother would recover.

The mother praised the doctor for the things that he had done, But the doctor said she would have died had it not been for her little one.

"How proud you must be of your little girl," he said. "It was her pleading that made me come."

"But doctor," the woman said, "my daughter died over three years ago. That's her picture on the wall."

The doctors legs went limp for the picture on the wall was of the little girl who had come to his office.

The doctor stood motionless for quite a little while, and then his solemn face was broken by a smile. He was thinking of that frantic knock heard at his office door and of the beautiful little angel that had walked across his floor.

Only You

You may only be one person in the world,
but to one person you may be the world.

Thank You, Lord

A preacher said to a precocious six-year-old girl. "So, your mother says your prayers for you every night. That's wonderful! What does she say?"

And little Sage replied, "Thank God she's in bed!"

When I Say . . .

When I say "I am a Christian,"
I'm not shouting "I am saved."
I'm whispering "I get lost!"
And that is why I chose this way.

When I say "I am a Christian,"
I don't speak of this with pride.
I'm confessing that I stumble
And need someone to be my guide.

When I say "I am a Christian,"
I'm not trying to be strong.
I'm professing that I'm weak
And pray for strength to carry on.

When I say "I am a Christian,"
I'm not bragging of success.

I'm admitting I have failed
And cannot ever pay the debt.

When I say "I am a Christian,"
I'm not claiming to be perfect.
My flaws are all to visible,
But God believes I'm worth it.

When I say "I am a Christian,"
I still feel the sting of pain.
I have my share of heartaches,
Which is why I seek His name.

When I say "I am a Christian,"
I do not wish to judge.
I have no authority.
I only know that I am loved.

God Explains

If you never felt pain,
Then how would you know that I'm a healer?

If you never went through difficulties,
Then how would you know that I'm a deliverer?

If you never had a trial,
How could you call yourself an overcomer?

If you never felt sadness,
How would you know that I'm a comforter?

If you never made a mistake,
How would you know that I'm forgiving?

If you knew everything,
How would you know that I will answer your
questions?

If you never were in trouble,
How would you know that I will come to your
rescue?

If you never were broken,
Then how would you know that I can make you
whole?

If I gave you all things,
How could you ever appreciate them?

If I never corrected you,
How would you know that I love you?

If you had all the power,
Then how would you learn to depend upon Me?

If your life was perfect,
Then what would you need Me for?

A Sack Of Potatoes

A teacher once told each of her students to bring a clear plastic bag and a sack of potatoes to school. For every person they had refused to forgive in their life's experiences, they were told to choose a potato, write on it the name of the person, and put it in the plastic bag. Some of the bags were quite heavy.

They were then told to carry this bag with them everywhere they went for one week, putting it beside their bed at night, on the car seat when driving, and next to their desk at school.

The hassle of lugging around this bag soon made it clear to them what a weight they were carrying spiritually, and how they had to pay attention to it at all times . . . how they could not forget it or leave it in embarrassing places.

Naturally, the condition of the potatoes deteriorated to a nasty slime. This was a reminder of the price we pay for keeping our pain and negativity. Too often we think of forgiveness as a gift to the other person. Clearly, it is for ourselves!

Sound Advice

Little feet stomp overhead,
Jumping, laughing, they romp
Resisting bed.

"Shhhhhhh! Quiet now!"
she calls.
Time for only the house to speak.

Silence descends,
Floorboards creak.
Time for only the house to speak.

How much time has passed from scene to scene.
The leaves have turned
From brown to green.

Her hair,
Once a shimmering crown of gold,
Has taken a cast reserved for the old.

123

The voices she quieted have grown and gone.
Still they speak.
Willing them not to be still now she closes her eyes
And longs for what she has known.

Come back little feet,
Romp and stomp from bed to bed.
Dance your patter above my head.

Then a ruckus at the door.
Calling voices, doorbell rings,
"Grandma, Grandma," the voices sing.

Young mother struggles
To them contain,
Her face showing a familiar strain.

"Shhhhhhh, quiet now,"
comes Grandma's tone.
Soon enough you'll be alone.

Listen to the music of your child's call.
Footfall running down the hall.
Weeping, leaping, soon enough we'll all be sleeping.

Best not to slumber while we are awake.

Don't Worry About It

Little Erica was kneeling by her bed and saying her prayers, and she asked God to make her be a good girl.

The girl's mother, passing by the bedroom, overheard her daughter praying: "And make me a good girl if You can. And if You can't, don't worry about it, because I'm having fun the way I am."

Friends For Life

In kindergarten your idea of a good friend was the person who let you have the red crayon when all that was left was the black one.

In first grade your idea of a good friend was the person who went to the bathroom with you and held your hand as you walked through the scary hallways.

In second grade your idea of a good friend was the person who helped you stand up to the class bully.

In third grade your idea of a good friend was the person who shared their lunch with you when you forgot yours.

In fourth grade your idea of a good friend was the person who was willing to switch square dancing partners with you during gym class.

In fifth grade your idea of a friend was the person who saved a seat in the back of the bus for you.

In sixth grade your idea of a friend was the person who asked a guy you liked to dance with you.

In seventh grade your idea of a friend was the person who let you copy their social studies homework.

In eighth grade your idea of a friend was the person who helped you pack up your stuffed animals so your room would look like a "high schooler's" room, but didn't laugh when you finished and burst into tears.

In ninth grade your idea of a good friend was the person who went with you to that "cool" party thrown by a senior so you wouldn't have to be the only freshman there.

In tenth grade your idea of a good friend was the person who changed their class schedule so you would have someone to sit with at lunch.

In eleventh grade your idea of a good friend was the person who gave you rides in their new car, convinced your parents that you shouldn't be grounded and found you a date for the prom.

In twelfth grade your idea of a good friend was the person who helped you pick out a college, assured you that you would get into that college, and helped you deal with your parents who were having a hard time adjusting to the idea of letting you go.

Now your idea of a good friend is still the person who gives you the better of two choices, holds your hand when you're scared, helps you fight off those who try to take advantage of you, thinks of you at times when you are not there, reminds you of what you have forgotten, helps you put the past behind you but understands when you need to hold onto it a little longer, stays with you so that you have confidence, goes out of their way to make time for you, helps you clear up your mistakes, helps you deal with pressure from others, smiles for you when you are sad, helps you become a better person, and most importantly loves you.

Not His Job

A passenger jet was suffering through a severe thunderstorm. As the passengers were being bounced around by the turbulence, a young mother with a small child on her lap and obviously frightened turned to a minister sitting next to her.

"Reverend," she asked with a nervous laugh, "you're a man of God. Can't you do something about this storm?"

To which he replies, "Lady, I'm in sales, not management."

Tasty

Life is short.
Eat dessert first.

Old Shoes

I watched him playing around my door,
My neighbor's little boy of four.
I wondered why a boy would choose
To wear his dad's old worn-out shoes.

I saw him try with all his might
To make the laces snug and tight.
I smiled to see him walk and then
He'd only step right out again.

I heard him say, his voice so glad
"I want to be just like my dad."
I hope his dad his steps would choose
Safe for his son to wear his shoes.

And then a shout and a cry for joy
A "Hello, Dad" and a "Hi-ya, boy."

They walked along in measured stride.
Each face aglow in love and pride.

"What have you done today, my lad?"
"I tried to wear your old shoes, Dad.
They're big, but when I am a man
I'll wear your shoes, I know I can."

They stopped and stood there hand in hand.
He saw his son's tracks in the sand.
His word, a prayer, comes back to me.
"Lord, let my steps lead him to Thee."

It's In Your Heart

There was this little girl sitting in the park one day. Everyone passed and never stopped to see why she looked so sad. Dressed in a worn pink dress, bare foot and dirty, the girl just sat and watched the people go by. She never tried to speak. She never said a word.

A young woman who had noticed the girl went back the next day to see if the child would still be in the park. And sure enough there she was in the same spot with the same sad look upon her face.

The woman went to speak to the little girl, but as she drew close she noticed her dress was strangely misshapen. That was the reason people hadn't stopped. The girl was severely deformed.

The woman smiled at the child to let her know that everything was OK...that she was there to help, to talk. The woman said, "Hello," and after awhile the girl stammered "Hi." They began to talk and stayed until darkness fell and the park was completely empty.

The woman asked the child why she was so sad. And the girl replied, "Because I'm different."

"Little girl," the woman said, "you remind me of an angel, sweet and innocent."

The child looked at the woman and smiled. Slowly she got to her feet and asked, "Really?"

"Yes," the woman answered, "you're like a little guardian angel sent to watch over all those people walking by."

The girl shook her head and said, "Yes," and with that she spread her wings.

With a twinkle in her eyes, she told the woman, "I am a guardian angel. I'm your guardian angel."

The woman was speechless, not sure of what she was seeing. "Why did no one stop to help an angel," she asked the girl.

The girl looked at the woman and smiled. "You're the only one that could see me. That's because you believe. You thought of someone other than yourself. It's in your heart. My job here is done." And then she was gone.

Happiness Is . . .

Taking in all the wonders of life,
its joys, its sorrows, its sunshine, its smiles.
Learning from the experiences each one brings you,
and then, from a caring heart,
giving them all away again.

Truisms Of Life

Conscience is what hurts when everything else feels so good.

Talk is cheap because supply exceeds demand.

It's easier to fight for one's principles than to live up to them.

Even if you are on the right track,
you'll get run over if you just sit there.

The Most Beautiful Flower

Disillusioned with life
with good reason to frown,
for the world was intent
on dragging me down.

And if that weren't enough
to ruin my day,
a young boy out of breath
approached me, all tired out from play.

He stood right before me
with his head tilted down
and said with excitement,
"Look what I've found."

In his hand was a flower,
what a pitiful sight,

with its petals all worn,
not enough rain or too little light.

Wanting him to take his dead flower
and go off to play,
I faked a small smile
then shifted away.

But instead of retreating
he sat next to my side,
placed the flower to his nose
and declared with surprise.

"It sure smells pretty
and it's beautiful, too,
that's why I picked it;
here, it's for you."

The weed before me was
dying, or dead.
not vibrant of colors,
orange, yellow or red.

But I knew I must take it,
or he might never leave,
so I reached for the flower and said,
"Just what I need."

But instead of him placing
the flower in my hand,
he held it in mid-air
without reason or plan.

It was then that I noticed
for the very first time
that weed-toting boy could not see:
he was blind.

I heard my voice quiver,
tears shone like the sun,
as I thanked him most humbly
he took off in a run.

I sat there and wondered
how he managed to see
a self-pitying old woman
beneath an old willow tree.

How did he know
of my self-indulged plight?
perhaps from his heart
he'd been blessed with true sight.

Through the eyes of a blind child,
at last I could see
the problem was not with the world
the problem was me.

And for all of those times
I myself had been blind,
I vowed to see the beauty in life
and appreciate every second that's mine.

And then I held that wilted flower
up to my nose,
and breathed in the fragrance
of a beautiful rose.

And smiled as I watched that young boy,
another weed in his hand,
about to change the life
of an unsuspecting old man.

Get Yourself Out Of The Way

It is when we forget ourselves that we do
things that are most likely to be remembered.

Love Always

Grace went to her mailbox and found just one letter. But, there was no stamp, no postmark, just her name and address on the envelope. She read the letter.

Dear Grace,

I'm going to be in your neighborhood Saturday afternoon and I'd like to stop by for a visit.

Love always,

Jesus

Her hands were shaking as she placed the letter on the table. "I don't have anything to offer," she thought, as she remembered her empty kitchen cabinets. "I will have to run to the grocery to find something for dinner."

Grace reached for her purse and counted out five dollars and 40 cents. "Well, I can get some bread and cold cuts, at least," she said as she threw on her coat and hurried out the door.

A loaf of French bread, a half-pound of turkey and a carton of milk was what she bought, leaving her a grand total of 12 cents until Monday. Nevertheless, she felt good as she headed home, her meager offerings under her arm.

"Hey, lady, can you help us?" Grace hadn't noticed the two figures huddled in a doorway. There was a man and a woman, both of them dressed in little more than rags. "Look, lady," the man said, "I'm out of work and my wife and I haven't eaten for days. Can you spare something?"

"Sir," Grace said, "I'd like to help you, but I'm a poor woman myself. All I have is a few cold cuts and some bread and I'm having an important guest for dinner."

But as the man turned away, Grace felt a familiar twinge in her heart. She ran after him and said, "Here take my food, I'll figure something out."

Grace also could see how the man's wife was shivering. "Here, take my coat, too," she said. "I have another coat at home." The man and woman said their thanks and moved on.

As Grace headed home she was chilled without her coat and also worried about what she was going to serve her Lord. Reaching home, she found another letter in the mailbox.

Dear Grace,

It was good to see you again. Thank you for the lovely meal and thank you, too, for the beautiful coat.

Love always,

Jesus

I'm Going! I'm Going!

A woman went into a pet shop and told the owner she wanted to buy a pet. But she didn't want any ordinary pet, she wanted a pet that could do everything.

The shop owner suggested a faithful dog. The woman rejected the idea.

The owner said, "How about a cat?"

"No way," said the woman, "a cat can't do everything."

The shop owner thought for a while, then said, "I've got it! A centipede!"

The woman said, "A centipede? I can't imagine a

centipede doing everything, but I'll give it a try." She took the centipede home and said to it, "Go clean the kitchen." Thirty minutes later, the kitchen was spotless.

Then she said, "Go clean the living room." Twenty minutes later, the living room was spotless also. Even the pillows on the sofas had been plumped.

The woman thought to herself, "This is the most amazing thing I've ever seen. This really is a pet that can do everything."

Next, she says to the centipede, "Run down to the corner and get me a newspaper."

The centipede walks out the door. Ten minutes later, no centipede! Twenty minutes later, no centipede! Thirty minutes later, no centipede. By this time, the woman was wondering what's happened. Forty-five minutes went by and no centipede. Did it get run over by a car? Was it eaten by a bird?

So she went to the front door, opened it, and there

was the centipede sitting right outside.
The woman said, "Hey, I sent you down to the corner
to get me a newspaper 45 minutes ago. What
happened?"

The centipede looks up and says, "I'm going, I'm
going! I'm just putting on my shoes!"

Top Ten Things Only Women Understand

10. Why it is good to have five pairs of black shoes.

9. The difference between cream, ivory, and off-white.

8. Crying can be fun.

7. Fat clothes

6. A salad, a diet drink and a hot fudge sundae make a balanced lunch.

5. Discovering a designer dress on the clearance rack can be considered a peak life experience.

4. The inaccuracy of every bathroom scale ever made.

3. A good man might be hard to find, but a good hairdresser is next to impossible.

2. Why a phone call between two women never lasts less than 10 minutes.

And the Number One thing only women understand:

1. Other women.

How Moms Were Made

At the time the Lord made mothers He was into the sixth day, working overtime. An angel appeared and asked, "Why are You spending so much time on this one?"

And the Lord answered, saying, "Have you read the spec sheet for mothers? She has to be completely washable, but not plastic; have 200 movable parts, all replaceable; run on black coffee and leftovers; have a lap that can hold three children at one time, which disappears when she stands up; have a kiss that can cure anything from a scraped knee to a broken heart; and have six pairs of hands."

The angel was astounded at the requirements. "Six pairs of hands? No way!" said the angel.

"Oh, it's not the hands that are the problem," replied the Lord, "it's the three pairs of eyes that mothers must have!"

153

"And that's on the standard model," the angel asked.

"Yep," said the Lord. "One pair of eyes is to see through doors when she asks what they are doing. Another pair in the back of her head are to see what she needs to see even though no one thinks she can. And, of course, the third pair is for the front of the head. They are for looking at an errant child and saying that she loves him or her without uttering a single word."

The angel tried to stop the Lord. "This is too much work for one day. Wait until tomorrow to finish."

"But I can't," said the Lord. "I'm so close to finishing this creation that is so close to my heart. She already heals herself when she is sick, and can feed a family of six on a pound of hamburger."

The angel moved closer and touched the woman. "But Bou have made her so soft, Lord."

"She is soft," the Lord agreed, "but she is also tough. You have no idea what she can endure or accomplish."

"Will she be able to think?" asked the angel.

"Not only will she think," the Lord said, "she will be able to reason and to negotiate."

The angel then noticed something and reached out and touched the woman's cheek. "Oops," the angel said, "it looks like You have a leak in this model. I told You that you were trying to put too much into her."

"That's not a leak," said the Lord. "That's a tear!"

"What's the tear for?" the angel asked. And the Lord replied, "The tear is her way of expressing her joy, her sorrow, her disappointment, her pain, her loneliness, her grief, and her pride."

The angel was impressed. "You are a genius, Lord.

You thought of everything. You even created the tear!"

The Lord looked at the angel and smiled, saying, "I'm afraid you are wrong again, my friend. I created the woman . . . but she created the tear."

155

He Began with Eve

Joyce Landorf Heatherley

BALCONY PUBLISHING

SALADO, TEXAS 76571

HE BEGAN WITH EVE

Library of Congress Cataloging in Publication Data

Landorf, Joyce.
  He began with Eve.

  1. Women in the Bible—Fiction.   I. Title
PS3562.A477H4   1983   813'.54   83-16673
ISBN 0-929488-12-1

Balcony Publishing, Inc. Paperback Edition
Copyright © 1990 by Joyce Landorf Heatherley

CONTENTS

ACKNOWLEDGMENTS

For the countless times these
people have helped and encouraged
me in the writing endeavors
of my life,
I'll be grateful forever.

Edward Peterman
Eunice Yoder   Virginia King
Azusa Pacific University

Francis Heatherley   Ernie Owen
Beverly Phillips   Floyd Thatcher
Word, Inc.

Brenda Arnold   Sharon Kite
Sheila Rapp   Artyce Homan
Personal Editorial Assistants

INTRODUCTION

In his very perceptive booklet, titled *Woman* (Multnomah Press, 1983), Charles Swindoll describes the mark of maturity a Christian woman *can* demonstrate in today's world. He says of her that she *can* be

> . . . freely alive;
> functioning to her maximum capacity;
> free to be who she is;
> yet willing to live within the God-given
> limits He has prescribed for the home.

His words beautifully describe what I *dream* of seeing in the lives of Christian women today—and what I have already seen in most of the women of the Bible.

This past year I've been teaching a series in my Thursday morning Bible class on some of those great Biblical women. And, for me, they have truly come alive. They are examples of women who had a sane estimate of personal worth, who earned love and respect, and who were clothed in an awareness of their sense of destiny and dignity.

These women were *real* and they were *responsible*.

REAL—in that they understood clearly *who* they were and

9

accepted God's evaluation of their personal worth and esteem.

RESPONSIBLE—for at the same time, while they were realistic women with enormous individuality, they *willingly* made themselves accountable to God for their actions. Consequently, they became great women of God.

I have chosen a number of them, and have written parts of their stories out in "novel" form. I wanted us to see their world from their eyes, and so, in effect, as I wrote I tried to become them. In the process I've developed a magnificent pride in the knowledge that I am a woman.

These Biblical women have also stirred up a deeply moving love in my heart for the Lord. After all, it was He who created the complex and yet glorious creature called female.

We women have been designed by the Master Designer, and it is my intense hope that as you read about these women, you will catch a shimmering glimpse of what God had in mind when He took a rib from man's breast, fashioned a woman around it, and then later, brought her to the man.

You and I were brought into existence that moment in time, but even today we need help to be the woman God wants us to be.

In the words of my friend Chuck's prayer,

Do give us new measures of grace. And a vast amount of mercy. And your matchless peace. May those spiritual gifts free us from panic and get us in tune with your Word so that everything false and phoney will be filtered out as discernment replaces gullibility. And may all this give us a maturity that restrains us from embracing error clothed deceitfully in the garb of truth. With quiet confidence we trust you.

So dear sisters in Christ, with that "quiet confidence" in our Lord, celebrate your God-created womanhood. Read of these magnificent women of Biblical times and see what God will reveal to you as you live now—in this complex world. And remember, He had *you* in mind when He began with Eve!

PART I

"And [God] brought her to the man."

Genesis 2:22

Quickly she moved through the immense and majestic forest. Only a few days before had she become aware of herself and her surroundings. All of it was still overwhelming, impressive, and completely captivating.

With her newly-formed curiosity cresting within her, she longed to stop, to explore, and to study the wonder and grandeur about her. Instead, a greater urging about the unknown before her pushed her along at a hurried pace.

The unseen *Presence,* for that's what she had named Him, was just ahead, leading her deeper and deeper into the magnificent forest. He was gently persistent in urging her onward.

In truth, even if she had wanted to—and she did not—the woman could have done nothing but follow. He had been irresistible even though she'd not actually seen Him.

From the beginning of her awakening, she had instinctively understood how she would respond to Him. Catching and holding Him to her inner being without seeing Him or knowing who He was came easily, for she had simply known He was *there* and was drawn instantly to Him.

Effortlessly this first eager learner scrambled over ground that had never before been trampled by human feet. Joyfully she skipped and skirted around billowy trees that had never provided shade to any traveler. And exhilarated, she waded through the shallow part of a mighty river in the middle of the forest which no person had ever crossed. Intoxicated by the Presence, the land, and the pace, she continued her journey.

Once, with her dark eyes dancing, she called out, "Now where are we going? And what new, surprising wonder do You have to show me?"

That the Presence hurried on without a word did not trouble her, nor was she afraid. In fact, her fledgling trust and deepening love for Him was so strong that girlishly she giggled when He gave her no clues as to the secret promises of that day.

At one place, when she passed close enough to a small, flowering tree, she managed to snatch one of its white-petaled blossoms. Quickly she tucked it in on one side of her dark, luxuriant hair.

Time was not a reality for her, and since she had no sense of its passing, she neither knew nor cared how long she had walked that morning. Only now, quite suddenly, she found herself standing still along the edges of the forest.

Just before her, past the last fringes of foliage and down a slight hill, stretched an exquisite meadow. The scene was in direct contrast to what she had just passed. Instead of huge, regal trees, the meadow grew only a few fragile trees here and there. The ground was covered with long, soft green grasses which were delicately sprinkled with tiny pale pink, warm violet, and soft yellow flowers. And here and there magnificent butterflies with rich paintings on their wings added bright, darting flashes of color.

Ahead of her the Presence was still, so she inhaled the fragrant beauty of the meadow and began to fill herself with the details and special wonder of this new place. Looking and exploring with her eyes, from the outer perimeter to the very center of the meadow, she was completely enchanted.

The meadow was set in a little valley, and fringed about with the dark green trees of the forest, it was so perfect she said aloud, "Presence, I'd like to stay here always . . . how wonderful it would be to sleep and wake in this meadow each day and night."

Then a happy thought came. "Did you make this place for me . . . was that Your intent all along?" She hoped she was right. "Is this Your gift to me? If it is, I shall lovingly care for it. How did You know I would love it so much?"

She would have carried on the one-sided monologue except she realized the Presence had slipped away, so she stopped. He'd return later. Now, she contented herself with giving full attention to her surroundings.

She began walking in the soft grass, still reveling in the wonder of her discoveries and picking some of the flowers. After a time she was startled by a sound which came from somewhere behind her.

It was a new sound. Something she'd never heard before. Someone's *audible voice* had called out a greeting to her, and she froze statuelike in surprise.

When she finally managed to move, she turned slowly around and found herself facing the source of the sound. Even though she had never seen the Presence, she knew this creature was not He. Also, she quickly reasoned that this being was not a part of the land, the river, or the sky. In truth, he did not remotely resemble *any* of the land or sky creatures she'd observed. He was unique from all others.

She felt no fear or shyness, so she stood tall and poised before him. Calmly she appraised him with both her eyes and her mind.

For a few awesome moments, they stood several paces apart and then, when he again found his voice, the man said, *"You are so beautiful."*

The sound of his voice intrigued and captured her all at the same time. It was deeper than the sound of the rushing river water and more winsome and noble than the voices of any of the creatures she'd passed in the forest or heard above her head in the trees. And while the other sounds she'd heard had been just that, sounds, his sound was different. What surprised her the most was that she had fully understood the sounds he'd uttered.

To be told she was beautiful pleased her above anything she had heard or seen in her brief existence. Without moving, her eyes recorded and took detailed notice of him, from his head to his feet. Then, in all truthfulness and simplicity, she acknowledged, *"You are beautiful,* too . . . but, even more, you are like this place. Absolutely *perfect."*

They were invisibly drawn toward each other, and as they came closer together, he shook his head, not in disbelief, but in sheer amazement and wonder as he watched her movement toward him. Then, aglow with pleasure, he exclaimed, seemingly more to the sky than to her, "This morning, at sunrise, God told me that He would bring you to me. That no more would I be alone without *my* kind. How could I have imagined that you would be *more* beautiful than all of this?" He waved his hand vaguely at the perfection which surrounded them.

"God?" she questioned.

"Yes. God . . . the one who made us," he replied.

"So that's His name!" The woman rolled the name over her tongue and then explained, "I called Him the 'Presence' because He was just . . . just with me. But His real name is God?"

The man nodded his head, once again saying, "Yes," and she found that his words richly satisfied the deepest part of her soul . . . so much so she gave him a dazzling smile. Intuitively she guessed that they both had pleased each other beyond measure. Her spirits soared within her, and the pleasure of the moment rebounded between them.

Bending down and forward slightly, the man put his arms around her and pulled her close to his body. His face glowed with pure joy, and she sensed his overwhelming love for her.

When, a moment later, he gently released her and regained his composure, he cradled the woman's face in his hands and with a gentle tenderness he whispered, "You are bone of my bones and the flesh of my flesh. I am you. You are me. And we are one."

Midmorning, on the day that was to forever change the course of all mankind, the man looked up from the plants and flowers in front of him and saw her making her way through the lush foliage toward him. As always his heart was smitten afresh with loving her, and, even though she'd only been gone a brief part of the morning, he had already begun to miss her. But, as he watched her, something about her walk or her look alerted a sense of vague uneasiness within him. Instantly he dismissed the thoughts, for the woman was as beautiful as she had been, and nothing had really changed. They were still one, he reasoned.

Readily they had come to accept that what was stirring in their souls was the beginning of a process. It was a process whereby two people, in great respect and love, would encourage, protect, strengthen, comfort, and share each other. Blossoming out of that maturing process came the flowering of their inevitable oneness.

Both of them were named *Adam* by God's design as though He wanted to ensure and preserve their unity. They were inseparable, united, and filled with a deep sense of wholeness.

Their days were crowded and crowned by intellectual achievements and artistic creativity. Together they explored the entire garden forest, discovered new animals and birds each day—and most fun of all, they named all the living creatures. And there, in the expansive beauty of forest and meadow, each dawn and sunset passed in marvelous activities and restful golden splendor.

Now as the woman came closer to him, he rose and laid aside his anxieties and reveled in her extraordinary beauty.

"What have you behind your back?" he asked as he smiled down at her.

"It's just some fruit I found," she said almost shyly.

There were still many trees and bushes laden with succulent-looking fruit just waiting to be tasted, so he said, "I see. So that's where you've been all morning . . . tasting and trying new fruits." Then he wondered why she was still holding her hands behind her and for some unexplained reason, his uneasiness returned. In fact, a definite feeling of apprehension began to tense his body.

A bit warily he asked, "Where in the forest did you find this?"

"It's from—" momentarily she halted. "It's fruit from the tree of knowing good and evil."

"What tree?" he gasped, even though he had clearly heard and understood her.

"The tree of knowing good and evil," she repeated.

Now the man's breathing became labored, yet he blurted out, "But God said—and we must *obey* Him—He told us not to eat of *that* tree!" He went no further because she had brought the fruit out from behind her and was now holding it up to him.

"You've *eaten* some of it!" he cried.

"Yes." She was puzzled by the tormented look in his eyes. Softly she continued, "It's very good . . . and see, nothing has happened to me. I want you to taste it, too."

"But," the man's face was ashen as he spoke, "God said if we ate of *that* fruit we would be doomed to die." In a daze he turned from her and began walking to the river.

"Adam," she called out, as she scrambled along behind him. "Adam, listen. Nothing has changed. See? I'm still the same. Besides, do you know exactly what it means to die?"

He stopped charging through the forest, turned, and faced her. "I . . . I . . . really don't know about dying; . . . only God said . . ." He stared at the fruit in her hands and stammered, "Maybe 'to die' means that when the sun settles over there behind those mountains" (he looked westward), "it won't come up in the morning. Or maybe dying means to live here but without the sun ever shining at all . . . or, maybe it means that we just go away and somehow not 'be' anymore. Oh, I don't know. I really don't know *what* God meant."

He moved on toward the river.

"Well, *whatever* it means," she whispered with a small degree of confidence, "the serpent said that even if we *did* eat this fruit, we *surely* wouldn't die."

Midstride the man stopped, turned, and almost shouted, "The serpent *talked* to you? None of the other creatures on the land, in the river, or in the sky talk, yet this one *speaks* and *reasons* with you?" he asked incredulously, his eyes wide open in astonishment.

"Oh, Adam, yes! And he is such a wise one. In fact, of all the creatures we've seen and named, he is the *most* beautiful. Come with me, and I'll find him again so you can see for yourself."

But Adam shook his head and dropped down onto the edge of the river bank. He dangled his feet in the rushing current and held his head in his hands. Nothing she said was making any sense and nothing was going to make him leave this spot by the river until he'd sorted things out a bit.

Desperate to understand, he looked up at her and asked, "Tell me, when you spoke with the serpent, did you think somehow that he was God? Did the serpent *sound* like Him?"

"Oh, yes," she said, nodding her head, "He *sounded* like

God at first. But soon I knew it wasn't He. However, I'm sure the serpent has met God and knows Him. And, as we talked, he convinced me that to eat of the fruit would be just fine . . . that nothing would happen or change in our lives."

Eagerly she explained, and then she coaxed, "Adam, my special love, see how fresh and lovely this piece is—please, eat some with me." She handed him what was left.

Adam's confusion was numbing his senses. She was his love. She was he. He was she. They were one. And he found he could deny her nothing. So, with a shrug of his shoulders, he ate what she had handed him.

The fruit was enormously delicious. The first taste mollified his confusion. It was true that he'd not eaten anything to equal its goodness. And, since he felt no change nor did he hear God's voice, he assumed that the serpent's words were true.

But his relief was short-lived. For as he looked up at the woman to tell her that he was all right and—as the serpent had suggested—perhaps God had not meant what He said, all his senses were suddenly assaulted by what he saw. He stared at her, not daring to believe his eyes.

The woman had been created by God and her beauty was divinely perfect. Adam had fallen instantly in love with her that first day in the meadow. But now, here, since eating the fruit, he could tell their disobedience had destroyed everything. The flawless, unblemished beauty of perfection he had seen in her and had so thoroughly enjoyed was gone. Simply gone. Vanished.

He scrambled to his feet, and in that moment, they both saw each other in a new way. Both of them were stunned. Extreme shame and embarrassment with their nakedness rolled over their souls like thick gray clouds of winter fog.

The first cold, dread feelings of fear overwhelmed them. They could not explain their inner responses—they could only acknowledge their existence. Neither one understood anything about themselves or the moment. Only later did they come to understand that on that day they had paid the highest price imaginable for their disobedience to God's instructions. That day also marked the moment when they began to understand the term, *to die.*

At first their nakedness frightened them and they did not know what to do about it. Then, seeing some soft leaves and stringlike vines, the idea came to cover themselves. Hastily, even clumsily, they tied on their first articles of clothing. Strangely enough, being clothed brought only a small comfort in those first fragile moments of living with their new awareness of each other.

Always before, in the cool of the evening—just after the sun had disappeared but while twilight still gently bathed their surroundings—they had waited expectantly for God's visit. But on this day of disillusionment and bewildering knowledge, they were even unaware of the sun setting until they heard God walking through the forest.

Their sundown time with Him had been the very center-piece of their existence. Always before they reveled in shar-ing their daily experiences and found answers to the many questions which flooded their minds. And, more often than not, because of their deepening friendship, their conversa-tions sparkled with loving laughter.

The joy produced by these rendezvous with their Maker and the camaraderie which was born in that special paradise knew no limits.

But now things were unmistakably changed. Their fear and panic were instantaneous. How could they face Him? Where could they go? Stricken with guilt and fear, they frantically ran through the great forest together, trying to find some hiding place to postpone, or even avoid their encounter with God. What had been the joy of their day now came as the curse of their lives.

"Adam, Adam—" God called. "Adam, where are you . . . and why are you hiding?"

Fright moving into terror, the man and woman clung to each other.

"Adam?" God called again. "Why are you hiding?"

The man's throat was caught in the paralysis of guilt and it seemed to take forever before he could answer.

As if it were indelibly written across their hearts and minds, the man and the woman never—in their hundreds of years of existence—ever forgot their idyllic life in Eden's paradise. Nor could they ever put out of their memories the last moments with God before their banishment.

Fearing the worst, and clinging to each other, the human pair were invisibly led by their Creator to the gigantic gates at the edge of their perfect world. There they stood, unable to quiet the incessant trembling of their bodies, as they heard the terms of their punishment.

Their Maker, thundering in tones of fiery wrath, first pronounced a curse upon the serpent. The two humans listened in petrified silence as they learned that no more would this creature be beautiful. In fact, from this fateful moment on, the snake would be set apart from all other animals. It was to be limbless and would crawl on its belly in the dust forever. The serpent was condemned to be the object of scorn and hatred by the woman and her offspring.

God's voice, now tumultuous like the roaring of a great lion, ended His curse to the snake with the powerfully prophetic words about the woman's offspring. "He shall bruise your head and you shall bruise his heel."

The woman had no comprehension as to what God had meant by "offspring" nor had she ever heard Him speak in such wrath. But, she had no time to sort it out or make sense of it, for suddenly she realized that God was talking directly to her.

"You shall bear children in intense pain and suffering," He was saying, "Yet, even so, you shall welcome your husband's affections, and he shall be your master." The woman and even the great forest were still for a moment as she absorbed the impact of His words.

"What did He mean? Bear children? In pain? What is pain?" she asked herself. *"What have I done that is so terrible it evokes such judgments and curses?"* she questioned as all her thoughts swirled and panicked in her head.

In the next moment it became the man's turn. Now God's voice, no longer thundering, was filled with naked anguish, and the awesomeness of His utterances was heard by all the living creatures.

Again an expectant stillness settled over the forest and God declared, "Because you listened to your wife and ate the fruit when I told you not to, I have placed a curse upon the soil. And Adam, all your life you will struggle to extract a living from it. It will grow thorns and thistles for you, and you shall eat its grasses. Until your dying day you will sweat to master it."

The man revived a moment from his shock and disbelief to ponder what "your dying day" meant. But then God went on. "You will return to the ground from which you came. For you were made from the ground, and to the ground you will return."

"Now," the man reasoned, "I think I understand." To the woman, still shivering in his arms, he whispered, "To die means to stop living. It means we go back to what we were *before* God made us. To be the dust of the earth once more."

God had finished now and the forest began to come alive with all the old familiar sounds of earth and sky creatures. But the two human beings scarcely heard them.

Adam, the man, looked deeply into the eyes of the woman he held. Then, he carried out his first official act of dominance and named her Eve. Instantly he was filled once more with his overwhelming love for her, and he pulled her even closer.

"Eve, Eve, my love." Softly he called her by her new name. "I have called you Eve," he explained, "because it means 'life-giving' and you are destined to become the mother of all mankind."

But her shattered spirit could not be mended, her tears would not stop flowing, and her body could not cease its tremblings.

In what was left of the daylight by the last traces of the sunset, the man and the woman remained locked in each other's embrace. Yet, in the deepening darkness, they were gradually aware of God's return and His activity.

To their astonishment they realized that God was fashioning, out of animal skins, what appeared to be coverings for them. In a few moments, Adam and Eve were outfitted. Gratefully they accepted the skins. The embarrassment they felt over their nakedness and the inadequate leaf coverings was still strong, but now because of the skins it had eased.

The humbling gesture of God, tailoring coverings for them to wear, was taken as an omen—a good omen. And they glimpsed their first ray of hope. Whispering excitedly they voiced their optimism.

"Perhaps His making clothes for us means He still cares?" Adam ventured.

"Maybe He will change His mind and rescind all the curses," Eve proposed, her eyes bright with the thought.

Eagerly now they exchanged ideas.

But God *could not* go back on His word. Disobedience had its price. There was no last minute reprieve and no changing of His mind. And all Adam and Eve's high expectations disappeared as they heard God question Himself aloud. "Now that man has become as We are, knowing good from bad, what if he eats the fruit of the Tree of Life and lives forever?"

They waited as His words echoed away.

But, as soon as they saw the mighty angels with the great flaming swords, they knew. It was over. He had decided to carry out His plan and now there was no going back.

"No, no!" they cried in unison, but God held firm.

Stumbling over their own feet in the deepening darkness of the evening, they were led to the extreme edge of the forest.

There God expelled them forever from the vast paradise. Angels took up their vigilant guard at the massive gates near to the Tree of Life, and Adam and Eve now understood fully the term "to die."

Life as they knew it was over. It was all over. Sobbing and terrified, with their arms clutching each other, Adam and Eve left their bright, completely perfect existence in the Eden of their innocence to enter the cold, dark realities of guilt in a stormy, turbulent world.

Soon after they were expelled from the great forest— or the Garden of Eden—as they later called it, Eve gave birth to their first child, a son named Cain. Following closely came a second son, and he was named Abel.

It seemed to Eve that with the passing of only a few moons her childbearing times came regularly and painfully down upon her. Sometimes one birth brought multiple babies which came in twos and threes.

At first she was mystified by the changes in her swollen body, fearful of the unknown and terrified of the actual pain of childbearing itself. But, after she had lived through fifty or sixty birthing experiences, it was only the pain she could never properly prepare herself to endure, nor strangely enough, remember when it was over.

Both she and Adam watched their children as they grew and paid close attention as they matured into adulthood. They had no way of knowing what to expect because they were the first husband and wife to experience the mysterious wonders of parental love. Often Eve remarked to Adam how the pure innocence of their children brought a measure of joy to her. And both parents sensed early in their earthly existence that a child's love could bridge almost any gulf and heal even the deepest of wounds.

Eve was filled with great expectations for all her children, but she watched none of them more closely than her first two sons—Cain and Abel.

Cain grew into manhood and, to Eve's mind, because he was her firstborn, he was somehow set apart. Special. And she took great delight in him.

Indeed, seeing Adam and Cain, father and son, as they tilled and coaxed the stubborn soil into giving back some of its life-giving sustenance, she was filled with a deep sense of satisfaction. No matter how many other sons worked the soil with Adam, Eve's mind always saw their firstborn side by side with his father.

Abel captured Eve's heart in a different manner. Even while he was little, he had a way with animals and seemed happiest when mothering some orphaned lamb or gently steering some cows or camels to a new pasture. Eve saw her own face and sensitive heart in Abel, and saw traits of God when the boy became a caring shepherd-man.

At night, by their tent's cooking fire, Adam and Eve instructed their children with their continual telling and retelling of their beginnings and their earlier existence with God. Whether they were training their children properly or succeeding at parenting, they could never be completely sure. Neither of these first parents had any memories to draw upon. No childhood memories of mother, father, brothers, or sisters; and no comparisons or conclusions could be formed from their past heritages. They simply lived and spoke what they felt God wanted them to do in the nurturing of their children.

However, they seriously doubted their parenting skills one harvest time, some thirty or so years after they had begun their family. They were stunned and shaken to the core of their beings by their first devastating tragedy.

That particular harvest season both Cain and Abel brought forth their offerings for God as Adam and Eve had taught them. Cain's offering was made up of fruits and vegetables from his farm while Abel's was his newest and fattest lamb. Adam and Eve never foresaw that God would reject Cain's produce and accept Abel's lamb.

Eve was working with several of her daughters, drying wooly sheepskins for clothing, when one of the younger boys came running and screaming across the open field. When the child caught his wind and spoke his message, Eve could only stare, open-mouthed at her young son. Cain had committed a horrific deed against his brother Abel.

Running across a clearing and a newly planted field, Eve frantically searched for her husband. When she found him she gave him the bare essentials, for that was all she knew, and then she blurted out, "We fed Cain and Abel the same porridge. They slept in the same tents. We loved them both in their own individual ways. Why did Cain kill his brother? Why?"

On into the night these questions raged in Eve's mind. By the cold, early dawn's light, her mind had quieted, and she was now kneeling by Abel's stiffened body when Adam, looking out across the field, said, "Eve . . . Cain comes."

Eve rose up and slowly walked out to meet him. When she was within touching distance, she flung her words at him.

"You had no right to do this bloody deed. How *dare* you wrench the life out of your brother?" She went on and on with her accusations, her voice burning deeply into Cain's conscience. Then, before he could defend himself or reply, Eve sensed the answer within her.

"The serpent! Was the serpent there?" she asked.

"No," Cain's barely audible voice responded. "I was by myself. I alone am guilty."

"But I don't understand why! Why did you . . . do this?" Eve looked back up the hill to the mound which was Abel's lifeless body.

"I was angry at God," Cain's defense began. "He would not accept *my* offering, but He willingly received Abel's. My anger and hatred for both God and Abel took hold of me and so I . . . I . . . did this thing."

Eve looked at the hardening lines of rebellion around Cain's eyes and instantly saw a reflection of her own day of disobedience. She was painfully stabbed with the memory that remained of her own devastating actions. The inner wounds had not healed.

Then, in a voice so low Eve had to bend forward to hear, Cain described his conversation with God which had occurred immediately after he'd killed his brother. In a flat monotone voice, drained of emotion, Cain related God's words and ended by telling his mother of the bargain struck between them insuring his physical safety.

Eve was not soothed nor did Cain's words help her through the quagmire of her grief. Bitter were the thoughts which welled up in her heart as she remembered the day God had asked the question, "Adam where are you?" Now today, He had asked a second question—"Where is your brother?" Then aloud, she wailed, "Oh what a waste! This wretched life is all sorrow."

Long after God banished Cain and they had buried Abel, Adam and Eve took long walks in the cool of the evening and mourned the loss of both sons.

Quiet settled in on Eve with a heavy finality. "It was my fault," she said over and over. "Even in the forest, way back then, it was my fault. And now this. This is my fault, too. I am the first sinner, and now look. My son follows."

Adam had volunteered very little as Eve put words to her grief, but when her grieving turned to heaping guilt on herself for Cain's heinous sin, he took matters into his own hands and declared with tender passion, "Eve, you must stop this. We have spent enough time going over and over our days in Eden. We have talked and reasoned about them. And while it is true that we, and we alone, were responsible for *our* disobedience, it is *not* true that you are responsible for Cain's choice. Our son was well into his manhood when he took Abel's life. He was not a child, but a man. He deliberately chose the unworthy offering for God and killed his brother. Now, like us, he pays for his disobedience." They had stopped walking, and Eve was absorbing Adam's words deep into her mind.

Adam continued, "Cain chose to do what he did, and it's not *your* fault . . . he chose the path he'd walk. Now, somewhere east of us, he lives . . . no, *survives* that awful moment of disobedience and sin. Eve, you must not carry this burden of despair. Remember, God has marked Cain so no one will kill him. So God must have a life for him to live. Yet, I know what you're feeling. None of this is what we dreamed of or hoped for."

Eve's heart began to move into a warmer chamber of acceptance. "It's the same now as the moments before our banishment, isn't it?" she asked. He nodded. "This is like the one moment of hope when God made our clothing from the freshly killed animals. Now, He marks our son—another moment of hope."

It was the last time she spoke of either of her two firstborn sons. It was as though she had reached some sort of a peaceable understanding about their fates.

From then on, neither Adam nor their children really knew how much Eve's soul grieved, or if she ever talked with God about the lost sons, Cain and Abel. It was a closed subject to those about her.

Each year she and Adam had more and more children, and they began to truly replenish the earth with their own kind.

It was when they were around 130 years old that Eve, right on her birthing schedule, had yet another child. The birth was routine as birthings went except that the moment she saw the child there was a quickening and stirring in her spirit such as she had not experienced in *many* years.

This perfectly developed man-child was unbelievably like Adam in every way. Eve gasped at the perfection of this beautiful child's countenance. Then, holding up his bare little body in front of her, she recalled with great clarity the day in the meadow of their paradise, when she had turned and seen Adam for the first time. This moment was like that one, and the beauty of it stunned her senses.

Instantly, she realized and fully understood that God was responsible for her joy, and that He had blessed her beyond measure with this new son. So she called the baby Seth, which meant "granted," for—as she put it to Adam—"God has *granted* me another son for the one Cain killed!"

Adam stood by, watching his beloved Eve as she held the newest of their babies. He sensed that though she rarely spoke of it, the rawness of the wounds of grief she carried all those years for the son who died and the one who went away were still very real and very painful.

Later that evening, after the baby Seth had nursed his fill, Eve called Adam to come and see the sleeping man-child.

"He is beautiful, like you," she whispered, "and what's more, he is God's gift to me." Eve bent over and gently kissed the baby's open hand.

Adam did not completely follow her line of talk, but he knew the moment was very special. His love for her still was so overwhelming that he drew her close, traced her face with his fingertips and said, "You are still *the* most beautiful gift of all."

With a radiant smile she dismissed his praise, and changing the subject she countered, "Please, Adam . . . I want to tell you about this extraordinary son of ours."

Her face was infused with a joy he could not ignore, so he said, "Then, tell me."

"Well," Eve began, "today as I held Seth, God surprised my heart by telling me that, of all our children, *this* son is of royal lineage. It is of his line and seed a savior . . . or a redeemer . . . will be born. You know, the one who will bruise the serpent's head . . . the one who will rule with justice.

"Oh, Adam, God's love and mercy poured over me today as I saw little Seth. It was such a magnificent feeling. Suddenly I was a young girl again, in the forest, running . . . running after the Living God, loving Him and knowing He loved me. And, Adam, as I spoke with Him, He gave me a hope in this child . . . a new, fresh hope . . . in this . . . our son Seth."

One could live without the soft blissful pleasures of Eden's paradise, one could live without a loved one (given enough time), but the truth which dawned on Adam and Eve that day was that one could not live without hope. Hope, even in the smallest of increments, was the only fuel for keeping the will to live alive.

Even in the dim light of the lamp, Adam could see that the tears of joyful reconciliation sparkled on her cheeks. *She has indeed made her peace with God. Today He has given us this child, a treasured child, to preserve the lineage of God,* Adam thought. Hope rekindled was once again burning within his wife and it was quite a sight!

The man's love for this woman raced through his veins exactly like it had so long ago when God brought her to him in the meadow of their beginnings.

PART II

Jochebed

"And Amram married Jochebed . . . and Aaron and Moses were their sons."

Exodus 6:20

*I*n the Hebrew sector of the sprawling Egyptian city of Helipolis, the burgeoning Israeli population was still sleeping. But soon men, women, and children would be plunged into their never-ending milieu of forced labor. And for hundreds of years it had been so. The Hebrews in this city had been relocated by Pharaoh from the land of Goshen, first established many years before by Joseph, and now they lived from sunup to sundown in this city shrouded in the gray cloak of hopelessness. No matter how clear and searing the Egyptian sun shone, nothing could warm their oppressed spirits or add the light of joy to their eyes. "Nothing will ever change the Pharaoh . . . it will always be this way," they murmured with resignation.

Each of the children of Israel had his own particular horror story to tell about the brutalities committed by the overbearing Egyptian taskmasters in the course of their daily work. They labored ceaselessly building the walls of the treasure cities of Pithom and Raamses; farming the land; serving in homes and the palace as domestic help; and learning to make the hand-worked crafts, art objects, metal engravings, and stone carvings for which Egypt was so famous. No part of Egyptian life was without the benefit of Hebrew hands, backs, and mental dexterity.

In less than an hour, Jochebed would join the million or more other Hebrews as they made their way to their mentally taxing and physically brutal jobs. She had been unable to quell the surging waves of nausea within her, so she lay as still as possible and listened to the small sounds of the early hours. After a moment or two, she rose on one elbow and, looking across the room, checked her sleeping children. Satisfied that Miriam and Aaron were fine and well covered, she pushed her own covers into a pillow for the small of her back. She hoped she'd find some measure of comfort and a few more precious moments of rest. It didn't work.

"What troubles you?" Amram whispered sleepily into the dark tresses of her hair.

"It is nothing, my husband. Please go back to sleep."

He patted her fondly and turned over hoping to delay the moment of leaving this safe haven. "They expect me to fill those impossible quotas . . . next the Pharaoh will ask us to make bricks without straw," he muttered before his breathing became slowed and steady.

Jochebed lay quietly as the darkness was replaced by the dawn's glow. Their tiny one-room hut was already crammed and crowded, and now that she was with child again, she'd have to make room for one more. As she lay on her pallet, she recalled the first time she'd discovered she was going to be a mother, seven summer seasons ago when they still lived in Goshen. A faint smile crossed her lips as she remembered how bitterly she had complained to Amram.

"Our first child, like generations of Hebrew children, will be born and flung into the incessantly snapping jaws of the Egyptian crocodile!"

Amram had smiled to himself. His cherished, and now indignant, wife could never bring herself to use the word *slavery*, so she'd always found ways to call it by other names.

Her resentment toward the Egyptians was kindled and kept alive by the reports of friends and relatives who worked as slaves in the households of the Pharaoh and other noblemen. The women told tales of vast opulent riches and of the ease of life lived by the Egyptians at the Hebrews' expense.

"Justice, where is justice?" Jochebed's voice had shrilled. "When will we rise up and destroy these enemies who use us like animals? Is there no man among the sons of Israel to stand up and *demand* justice and freedom for our people?"

In the first year of their married life, Amram had been discreetly told by family and friends to keep his outspoken wife quiet. "Because," as they put it, "the sound of her ranting could reach the palace and the wrong ears might hear her. Then all of us would suffer even more." What they said was true, Amram admitted, but hushing Jochebed proved too large a task for the man who loved her.

However, everything changed for Jochebed with the birth of their first child. As any other Hebrew woman, she had been dearly pleased when she realized she was with child. Bringing a baby into the world was believed to be one of *the* most tangible ways a woman felt a personal blessing from God. But pulling at her joy, from yet another direction, was her strong sense of rebellion and frustration at bringing a child into *their* world as they knew it.

This latter fear disappeared as soon as the midwife proclaimed that she had given birth to a whole and healthy girl-child. For at the same instant as the infant was lifted up for her to see, Jochebed heard another voice from deep within her—One who said, "It is only a matter of time now. I will rescue My people . . . and I will use *your* children to carry out My plans." She lay back on her pallet and pillows, dazed and not completely able to assimilate the full marvel of the message she'd heard. But she *had* heard the message, and hope charged through every vein in her body. Jehovah's words changed her and a whole new thought process began in Jochebed's mind.

The infant girl was named Miriam. Then, several years

later, God really smiled on Jochebed, and to her enormous joy a son, Aaron, was born. But it was from the moment she heard God's promise at the birth of her first-born that Jochebed was a different person.

Relatives and friends alike whispered and gossiped about the new Jochebed as she enthusiastically attacked her weaving work for the Egyptians. Much to even her surprise, she became cheerful as she willfully and steadily developed her skills in plaiting the river reeds and papyrus into all kinds of baskets. Also, to those who knew her, her change from being bitter and carping was astounding, and they wondered at the source of her mysterious inner peace.

The change was so apparent that several mothers and their daughters found themselves confiding in Jochebed and seeking out her wisdom on various subjects. She became close friend, wise teacher, and steady encourager to many.

Only Amram knew what had brought about this change of attitude, for one night, shortly after Miriam's birth, Jochebed revealed the secret promise of God which had pumped hope into every part of her being. Together they wondered about the hows and whens of God's plan.

Now it was time for Jochebed to give birth to her third child, and God had begun to reveal His plans for rescuing the Hebrew people from their bondage. Only no one, including Jochebed, recognized or perceived it as such.

Over the years Pharaoh's consternation about the rapidly multiplying Hebrew population had grown intensely. His worst fears were being realized. He simply *knew* that the Hebrews would continue to add to their numbers in this incredible fashion, outnumbering his own people, and then they would eventually revolt and take over all of Egypt.

So, with mounting panic, Pharaoh issued an edict. It was a devastating proclamation which ordered all Hebrew male babies to be thrown into the crocodile-infested waters of the Nile—either to be eaten alive, or to die by drowning.

The edict crashed down around Jochebed's heart like an avalanche from a stone mountain, for her God-given intuition had already firmly told her that the life she was forming within her was indeed a man-child.

The sounds of weeping and wailing, which came from grieving mothers, had assaulted the night air every night during the last few weeks of her confinement. Pharaoh's edict struck Jochebed's heart with loud, deafening chords of confusion and frustration.

"Why would God give me such a clear-cut promise and then let Pharaoh do this terrible thing? Have I so thoroughly misunderstood what God told me at Miriam's birth?" She poured out her questions, with much weeping, on Amram's shoulder. "I *believed* that secret message of hope . . . but, now . . . now, *what* do I believe?"

Her husband tightened his grip around her. He was powerless to change anything, and too sick at heart to say anything.

Jochebed continued, her voice rising with anger. "How could God use our children to rescue the Hebrew nation if the man-child I carry is *already* doomed to die?"

Daily anger and doubt plagued her, and by the time her waters broke and gushed from her and the pain of birthing bore down on her, Jochebed was drowning in the sea of despair. "I have no hope," she stated flatly.

Hours later, spent and exhausted, she shut her eyes tightly, pushed down hard, stifled a scream for the last time, and a baby boy burst forth into the waiting midwife's hands.

"Oh, Jochebed, look. . . ." It was Sarah. Dear Sarah. She was a friend and the number one apprentice to Shiphrah, one of the chief midwives of the Hebrews. Sarah was now calling Jochebed back from the pain which would at any moment engulf her. "Look, little mother, see your son. How beautiful he is!" Sarah said affectionately.

Jochebed's mind finally began to clear as her body started reviving from the raw pain and dark fatigue of childbirth. She sank back on her pillows, and motioning to Sarah, opened up her arms.

"All your children are special," Sarah whispered as she laid the newborn against Jochebed's breasts. "But this one . . . ah, this one is a treasure from God." Sarah was speaking out of a reservoir of hundreds of birthing experiences with her teacher, Shiphrah, and Jochebed could not treat her comments lightly. Carefully she looked at her little son.

Even in her after-birth haze, there was no denying that this was a beautiful child and somehow he seemed different from other babies. Faintly, beating in her soul, she began to hear the first cadence of the song of hope.

Perhaps, she thought, *perhaps God will, in SPITE of Pharaoh, use my children, and especially THIS child, for our deliverance just like He promised.* It was then, as she held her baby close and kissed his head, that she made her first deliberate decision concerning his future.

Reaching over and taking the midwife's hand she said, "Sarah, I'll not let Pharaoh have this one! We must not let him be taken from us. I don't know how to conceal him, or how to carry on with our labors and life, but somehow I'll find a way. Will you help me?" The midwife nodded in agreement, and the two women, in the dim light of the oil lamp, vowed, conspired, and grew exceedingly hopeful together.

Amram returned home after his labors and was met by a sparkling-eyed Miriam. "Father," she whispered, "I have another beautiful brother!" He rushed to Jochebed's side.

"Dearest, look." Then quietly but almost fiercely she said, "I will keep this child away from the river. The river will never claim him. He will never go *near* the river." Her husband was to hear her vow over and over again that first night.

With the coming dawn and a surging of new strength filling her mind and body, Jochebed's plans began to crystallize and take shape. Eagerness and anticipation burned brightly within her as she devised the strategy which would hide her baby for most of his infancy.

Saving his life became her life's highest priority. But the first three months were unquestionably the hardest. Somehow Jochebed managed the Herculean task of daily basket weaving for her Egyptian masters, fixing meals, and tending to her family's needs while simultaneously nursing, caring for, and hiding a sometimes-sleeping, sometimes-crying newborn. And it was all accomplished without attracting the attention of any Egyptians.

The baby, still unnamed as yet, was about three months old when Jochebed began to run out of ideas to assure and prolong his concealment. She knew she had to make some changes, but what? How?

As was her custom, she prayed as she wove the wet, flexible reeds into baskets. And, on this particular morning, it was just as she was into her oft-repeated prayer, "Protect him from above, oh, Great Jehovah, and I shall keep him away from the river . . ." that she distinctly heard the question in her heart, *Why NOT the river?*

And though she was terrified of the Nile and all it meant to her baby, Jochebed was instantly smitten with excitement at the thought. *That's right!* she said to herself. *What better place to hide my baby than in the river? It's perfect. What soldier or spy of Pharaoh would expect to find any baby, much less a Hebrew baby, along or in the Nile?*

Trembling with her joyful calculations, Jochebed forced herself to go calmly on with her basket weaving, for a few yards from her, two Egyptian overseers stood idly chatting. But Jochebed's call to Miriam was enough to alert the young girl.

"What is it, mother?" Her eyes asked if there was trouble.

"Everything is fine, just fine . . . and as soon as they leave. . . ."

When it was safe to talk and the Egyptians had moved on to inspect something else, Jochebed motioned Miriam to her side.

"Mother, are you all right?"

"Yes, yes, everything is fine, dear one." Jochebed smoothed away a small frown on Miriam's forehead. "It's just that Jehovah has given me another plan to save your baby brother." The girl's brown eyes glittered with excitement and she whispered, "How?"

"We'll use the river."

"The river?" Miriam's eyes widened in surprise.

"The river, my child. They will never look for a baby there . . . especially with you as my eyes and his protector."

Miriam, though she was only eight summers old, was a unique child who possessed a bright, quick mind and an equally quick sensitivity to others in her heart and spirit. Both she and her younger brother Aaron were eager to please their parents, but the girl's age and mental alertness gave her the edge.

Hiding her newest brother and keeping the family's secret came easily for her as she had fallen in love with him from the first moment she had seen him. The new baby had also kindled the spark of motherhood which lies beneath the surface of most eight-year-olds. In fact, up to the time of this baby's birth, Jochebed had always called her daughter "little Miriam," but upon seeing Miriam in action she was affectionately renamed "little mama." The name fit like a well-tailored tunic; it was appropriate, and it pleased Miriam immensely.

Now, as her mother talked, it grew increasingly difficult for Miriam to sit still. Her heart seemed to be thumping excitably in all directions, and she knew the days ahead would be filled with adventure. It would also be a change from the routine boredom of their daily tasks and existence.

In less than four days from the morning Jochebed eagerly whispered her intended plans to Miriam, the first part of the scheme was put into action.

Outside of her house, where Jochebed and several other women wove papyrus reeds into baskets, she chose a basket of medium size. It was the right length and depth to cradle a baby. Then, without slacking up on her other weaving so as not to call the attention of the overseer, she began layering this basket with tar and extra weavings of reeds. When Jochebed was satisfied that her craftsmanship had made the basket waterproof, and that it would stay afloat, she waited until dark and brought it into the house.

"You've made our baby a boat!" Miriam gleefully announced. And then, in motherly tones, she explained to Aaron, "Look! See, she has fixed it so the basket will stay on top of the water just like the big barges do." The children noisily examined their mother's creation with delight, and Amram shook his head in wonder. "What will that woman think of next?" he said proudly.

Very early the next morning, after the baby was bathed, had nursed his fill, and was fast asleep in his little basket-boat, Miriam carried him down to the river banks. Everyone, Hebrew and Egyptian alike were accustomed to seeing the girl carrying finished baskets to the Egyptian storage sheds where various supplies were stored. So the sight of Jochebed's daughter carrying a basket was as common as the sandy ground beneath her bare feet. That she walked *away* from the overseers' sheds and *toward* the river was not thought to be a matter of any important consequence.

The plan will work! Jochebed's thoughts sang to her as she watched Miriam walking very nonchalantly toward the river.

The spot where Miriam eased the basket into the river reeds was well chosen indeed. This place had been Miriam's choice, not her mother's, for in odd moments when she was not helping the women or running errands, she would slip away to this very place and wade in the soothing, tepid waters.

The thick massing of the bulrushes and various kinds of water reeds grew in profusion here like screens. And they provided the needed seclusion to ensure the baby's safety. It was the perfect place, too, because it was down-river away from the center of activity.

"And there, too, Mother," Miriam had excitedly volunteered, "the river is shallow enough that if a crocodile comes close I'll see him first!"

The child had remembered well her mother's words, "Watch for any unusual stirring the water makes, for, as you know, that's a sure sign that a crocodile is moving from one spot to another." The mother's lessons had been extensive, but the daughter's teachable spirit had caught on to all the aspects of the courageous plan.

"Now, let's say you see one of Pharaoh's men, do you know what I want you to do?" Jochebed had asked; and then, without waiting for Miriam to reply, said, "You talk to him about anything you can think of. And, as you talk, you lead him *away* from the baby's hiding place like mother birds do . . . *away* from their nest." The wide-eyed child had nodded solemnly.

"As for other children who might come to that spot on

the river—you tell them that this is *your* place to play. And should women come to wash their clothes or bathe themselves, quietly amuse yourself, pay attention to their conversations, and stay very close. Also, each day when the sun is directly over your head, bring the basket home, and I will feed him. After that, you can take him back to his hiding place and keep watch until the sun begins to go down behind the western hills."

Jochebed had tried to cover every detail of this momentous task with her daughter. Miriam was given one contingency and one supposition after another to try to prepare her for any eventuality she might face at the river. So it was that with her mother's patient teaching the child grew self-confident and quite equal to the task set before her.

"It's too heavy a burden for her . . . even if she is a 'little mama'," Amram said one night, some five days after Miriam's river vigil had begun. His eyes were dark with concern. "She's too young. What if she is overpowered or attacked by some evil Egyptian? Are we not in danger of losing both our daughter *and* our son?" He let the questions hang heavily in the hot night's stillness.

"You give me harsh words, my husband. Do you think I haven't asked myself these same questions in my own mind . . . over and over again?" Jochebed said, somewhat irritably. They rarely disagreed, but tonight, because they could no longer avoid the issues or sweep them away into a corner, they had to talk. So Jochebed continued, "Perhaps you are forgetting the power of the unseen Jehovah?" Amram had heard her speak like this before, and always her faith had outlived his skepticism. *She walks closely to Jehovah and hears Him more clearly than I,* his thoughts reassured him.

"Amram," she touched his arm, "my beloved. Just think . . . how can we *ever* understand the ways of Jehovah? His plans for our present or our future. . . ."

She sighed and then went on, "They are all hidden from us like a baby before he is born. Don't you suppose that Jehovah is powerful enough to blind the eyes of anyone who might come near our baby at the river? Or, He could turn the feet of an evil person in a different direction . . . but, can't you see that definitely, by some unknown way, He *could* protect the lives of both our children? Haven't we been told and retold the story of Jehovah's care and protection for Joseph when he first came to this very land?"

In the face of such practical logic and such determined faith, Amram felt himself relinquishing his fears. But still, with honesty, he said, "Jochebed . . ." He looked down at his calloused and sunburned hands. "What troubles me the most is that I cannot understand why Jehovah would protect and spare our children. And, yes, I know of the promise He gave you, but still, why would He choose to save *our* baby when He has turned a blind eye and a deaf ear to the saving of so many other Hebrew babies? You know that since the edict, hundreds of the sons of Israel have been sought out, found, and killed. Why is our son different—really?"

Amram's questions and rationale penetrated her soul like a sharp knife, and angrily she stared at him.

"I don't know why!" she cried shrilly, her face pale and waxen in the light of the oil lamp. "I only know that I believe our baby will survive. Somehow he will be spared. Jehovah promised . . . but I don't know *how* . . . only that Jehovah's rescue plans will be carried out by our children. And," she added determinedly, "I must do whatever I can to accomplish this." She spoke the words as if the telling would make them come true.

Their arguments in the past had always stayed at the dignified disagreement level. But the issue here was so life-threatening that both Amram and Jochebed forgot the presence of their children, their neighbors, and their captors. Their voices, heated and intense, filled the little house; and Jochebed, with a vexed and defensive spirit shouted, "I can't help it if I have only Jehovah's promise and not His battle plans!"

The touch of blasphemy in her words jolted Amram, and

he instinctively clasped his hand over her mouth. "Jochebed, hush! Others . . . *including* Jehovah, will hear you." Aaron and Miriam were now sitting up on their bed pallets, wide-eyed and frightened.

He was right and she knew it. Yet, somehow by speaking out and sharing their most frustrating anxieties her spirit had lost some of its fury and fiery inner smolderings; and now, with a cooler spirit, she said wearily, "Oh, Amram, it *will* be our children. Just think! *Our* children will lead the rest of the children of Israel into battle against our enemies. Is any sacrifice or risk too great to save our baby?"

She glanced over at Miriam and Aaron, and realized she needed to soothe their hearts. So, crossing over to their pallets, she crooned her oft-repeated goodnight song and assured them that all was well.

When the children were well settled, Amram silently motioned to her to come with him. As they stepped outside, the gentle river winds were up and they blew across their faces refreshing and renewing their tension-tight spirits. Slipping one arm around her shoulders, Amram pulled Jochebed down on the still-warm sand, and together they leaned back against their doorpost.

At first they wrapped themselves in their own thoughts and carefully digested the conversation that had preceded these moments. Silently they looked up at the dark star-filled Egyptian sky. Then Jochebed mused, almost as if to herself, "It's funny, but I've always seen myself as a mother bird to our children . . . I'd feed them, care for them, teach them how to fly. Then one day, only when I determined they were strong enough, I'd push them out of the nest and set them on their way. After all my training and loving, I'd *release* them to be the people Jehovah called them to be . . . I just never dreamed I'd have to release my little one at so tender an age. He is no more *near* ready to fly than I am ready to push him out of the nest . . . yet, I must."

Amram turned her face and, kissing her cheek, he

murmured, "You are remarkable . . . just remarkable . . . and what's more, you don't even know it. You've *already* released our little son into Jehovah's care, and tonight you've helped me to do the same. Actually," he said, as he gave a low chuckle, "you have released our beautiful little son into the care of Jehovah and an eight-year-old mother bird . . . both of whom will probably do a marvelous work." The humor and kindness which threaded through his words touched Jochebed deeply. And even in the darkness, Amram could see that her face was graced, and made more lovely, by a slight smile.

"Have you any idea of how long this could go on?" Amram asked of Jochebed one morning as Miriam was taking her special basket out the door. His frustration and fear were thinly veiled in the tone of his words.

Jochebed, with a small show of flippancy, retorted, "Well, should the baby outgrow his little boat I will just make him a bigger boat . . . and I'll do that for as long as I have to!"

"I mean," Amram sighed heavily, "when do you think it will be safe to take him from the hiding place and ease him into our family life . . . in two months, or what?"

Jochebed continued to fold up their night bedding, but

quietly she said, "My husband, please don't worry so. I know the days crawl slowly . . . making each one seem a lifetime. But, really, it's only been several days. Leave this in Jehovah's hands."

"I am a man who needs to *see* things . . . and, in this case, I do not *see* Jehovah's hands. Trusting doesn't come easily."

Leaving, he kissed her cheek. They both knew they would talk about it again. But Amram was supposed to be at work making the "impossible" bricks by sun up, and the pale light in the sky was quickly giving way to full dawn's brightness. "God watch between you and me," he called over his shoulder.

Midmorning, as Jochebed was putting the finishing touches on a small, intricately woven basket, Miriam came bursting into the tiny basket-lined courtyard. The two women working with Jochebed, Leah and Anna, stopped their chatter and their fingers to stare at the girl. Each woman's eyes asked the same question.

Jochebed kept her voice low but hissed, *"Where is your basket?"* "I left it at the river, Mother, but it's all right."

The girl answered easily in the simple code language they had agreed on. It was used, not for the women present, for they were both loyal Hebrews, but for any Egyptian who might overhear their conversation and discover their secret.

After she had caught her breath, and in a very grown-up voice, Miriam said, "They want to look at some of your baskets . . . at the river."

"They?"

"Yes, they. The Princess and her ladies." She wished her mother would stop asking questions and just *go* with her.

Jochebed cleared her throat and steadied herself against the front wall. "Pharaoh's daughter?" she gasped. Her eyes bore deep into Miriam's face as the child nodded. Leah had a furious attack of basket-weaving while Anna stared, round-eyed and open-mouthed.

As calmly as she could manage, Jochebed collected a few baskets and announced, "If you are asked . . . I'm at the river . . . ah, with the Princess." A still-frozen Anna mechanically nodded.

As they ran toward the river, Jochebed's heart was in her throat. "What is the daughter of the Pharaoh doing down here . . . at this place in the river?"

"She and her ladies were walking along the river banks . . . looking for a place to bathe . . . I think." Miriam answered.

"Have you ever seen her before?"

"No."

"She found our baby, didn't she?"

"Yes."

"How did that happen . . . why didn't you take him downriver?"

Jochebed was at once both proud and furious. She was proud and pleased with a daughter who had not panicked, but had behaved with a maturity beyond her tender years. However, she was furious with her own self for concocting this insane scheme in the first place. In her own panic, she began to doubt that Jehovah had been a part of this at all. Her heart had a hundred or more questions, but they were almost to the river's edge so she said, "Quickly, my child. Tell me all you can."

Miriam's words tumbled out, "I saw them first, so I tried to pull the basket farther into the reeds . . . but he woke up and started to cry. I knew they'd hear him, and they did, so I left him. I hid in the reeds, over there," she explained, pointing to a thick clump.

"Go on," Jochebed pressed.

"The Princess saw the basket and sent one of her maids to get it and—"Miriam never finished her sentence because suddenly, just before them was a group of beautiful, exquisitely-gowned Egyptian women. They were sitting on a thick elegant carpet while two slave girls waved enormous feather fans above their heads to stir the air and to provide a protective shade from the morning sun. It was a festive scene.

The women were clustered about Pharaoh's daughter who looked as if she were holding an informal court in the middle of them. Everyone was laughing, talking, and cooing at the baby who was sitting contentedly on the Princess' lap.

At that moment, the Princess saw the two Hebrews.

"Ah, child . . . I see you have found us a nurse. You are quick," the Princess said to Miriam. "I like that." She handed the baby to one of her ladies, stood up, and stepped off the carpet to get a better look at the woman. Her eyes had missed nothing. She noticed that the woman's milk had started to flow at the sight of the baby, and quickly it had stained her tunic with its wetness.

"Do you have an ample supply of milk in those breasts of yours?" the Princess asked anyway. Her inbred haughtiness did not offend Jochebed. In fact, Jochebed sensed that the baby's beauty and perfectly formed body had probably won the Princess' heart the instant she had seen him. And intuitively she also understood, in those moments, that the baby's survival was as much the Princess' intent as it was hers.

"Yes, my lady. As you can see, I have plenty." Jochebed smiled and covered the stain with her hands.

The Princess moved even closer to Jochebed, and with implied yet unmistakable intent, she said almost fiercely, "I want you to know, woman, that not *all* Egyptians are deaf to the cries of Hebrew children. Do you understand my meaning?"

Jochebed understood immediately. She marveled that Pharaoh's daughter had guessed her identity as the baby's natural mother, but had been clever enough to hide the fact in her conversation.

"Yes, my lady. I do understand, and," with her own clarity of intent she added, "I will loyally serve you, for I am humbled and grateful that the baby's cries reached *your* ears."

The slightest of smiles crossed the woman's classic Egyptian face. "Good!" She raised her voice now so the others could hear. "Now, take this child home with you. Nurse him and care for him. I will pay you well for your efforts. You will be released from whatever responsibilities you have to Egypt. From this time on, the baby is your only charge. See that you do not neglect or starve him. I expect you to treat him as your very own son." Her eyes flashed momentarily at Jochebed, and then she continued. "When he is older and completely weaned, bring him to me at the palace. From then on, he will be *my* son."

The Princess' heavily outlined eyes and cheeks were suddenly awash with tears. Quickly she turned her head and spoke so only Jochebed could hear. "I will love him as if he *were* my very own. He is the son I never had . . . do not fear for him, ever again. I will not allow him to be harmed."

Jochebed was stunned. She could only guess at the depth of the hurt behind the hastily spoken words.

Then, as quickly as the tears had come, the Princess' mood changed. She clapped her hands with a surge of joy, turned from Jochebed and, giving Miriam a quick hug, she called for the baby.

Eagerly she took him and announced, "Let's drink a toast to my beautiful little . . ." she tasted the word, *son,* before saying it aloud and found it delicious, so she fairly shouted, "My little *son* . . . Moses.

"Yes, that's his name—Moses—for I have drawn him out of the waters of the mighty Nile. Look at him! He is wonderful!" she sang, and her ladies chorused and echoed her words.

"He will be the great man of Egypt . . . someday, perhaps the greatest!" the Princess responded.

"No, he will be the great man of Jehovah," Jochebed silently said to herself. And then, dropping to her knees, she held

Miriam close and whispered, "Bless you, little mama. You were very wise and very brave today . . . oh, how I love you."

It struck every spring and every autumn like the fore-runner of the great plagues which were to pellet Egypt later in their lifetimes. This autumn was no different.

The burning, malignant fevers, commonly called "ague," moved over the people, especially those who lived near the riverbanks, and before the season was half over, hundreds had died of it. Their bodies quickly shriveled in the searing furnace of their white-hot fever.

So suddenly did the fever strike that on one autumn day, by the time fellow workers brought Amram home, his skin was too hot to touch; his face, blood red; and the ramblings from his mouth quite delirious.

As they laid him down, one of the men explained tersely to the tall, slim girl, "It's the fever. . . ."

By looking at her father Miriam knew instantly that this "fever" was the dreaded one, the fast one, and aloud she said, "It's ague." She had seen a number of kinsfolk die of this type of fever, but in all her nineteen years, it had never touched anyone in the house of Amram. Maintaining her poise, she quickly ran and got a basin of cool water. Then she took cloths, dipped them in the water, wrung them out, and began sponging off her father's fevered, red, swollen face.

Amram did not recognize his daughter, but even in the midst of his incoherent mumbling—he periodically called out for Jochebed. Over and over, each time a little more frantically, he called for his wife.

Trying to soothe him, Miriam said, "Sh, sh—it's all right, lie back . . . Mother is coming. She took some baskets to the overseers. She will be right back. Please, Father, leave the cloths on . . . you'll feel better. . . ." Miriam, not one given to fits of panic, struggled fiercely to change the wet material and to remain calm. She wished her mother would get there. She knew that her father's fever, which must have come on him suddenly this morning after he was already making bricks, was one of the most dreaded because it usually took its victims so quickly. Just at that moment, Aaron came through the doorway. "Find Mother!" she shouted, and without a word, her brother bolted out. Miriam knew that unless her mother returned soon, it would be too late. A shiver passed down her back.

Shortly Jochebed and several other women, breathless from running, came and crowded into the room. Jochebed flung herself across Amram. She was still kissing his mouth and crying, "Oh, no, no . . . no," when the last breath of life eased out of the dying man's chest.

Their little house was quiet in the days that followed Amram's death. The Egyptians took Aaron, now a strapping youth of sixteen, from his duties on the river barges and set him to making bricks, in his father's place. In dark, brooding silence Jochebed and Miriam went about their housekeeping tasks and basket weaving. Even when they went to the palace to tell Prince Moses that his father was gone, Jochebed gave the message in sparse detail and guarded language. Of the two women in the house, it was Jochebed, once so strong, who grew weaker and moved as a woman barely able to exist in the world of shattered dreams.

All this began to trouble Miriam. She worried about the

changes which were taking place in her mother. Then, a few moons after her father's death, Miriam attempted to draw Jochebed out of her quiet stagnation. First she tried to stir Jochebed's interest by small talk on her choice of food for the evening meal or the color of the setting sun— but the girl could hardly break through her mother's wall of inner silence. Nothing Miriam brought up or discussed seemed to bring back the sparkle to Jochebed's dark eyes.

Then, for reasons Miriam never knew or understood, Jochebed emerged from the shadows of her silence, and one night she slowly opened up her heart. At first her words came like a small trickle of water, but after awhile they broadened into a stream, and finally the pent up grief and loneliness poured and tumbled from her like a powerful waterfall. At last she was able to talk about the unspeakable day of Amram's death.

"When they brought your father home that day, did he say anything? Did he know you?" she asked.

The girl answered quietly, "No, I don't think he knew me. I didn't understand all the things he said, but he *did* ask for you."

Miriam, though still a young woman, put herself in her mother's place and sensed that Jochebed had been silently cold and withdrawn because she'd arrived home that dreadful day just a few minutes too late. The girl, observant and bright, could see that her mother's regrets and her "if only I had done . . ." thoughts had piled up within her like the stones of the great pyramids.

"Mother," Miriam encircled Jochebed with her arms, "Father asked only for you . . . he thought of no one else. The fever came so fast that he was almost gone before they brought him home. All you need to know and remember is that he loved you dearly . . . and he called out your name to tell you so."

Jochebed nodded her head and smiled faintly. Hesitantly she asked, "Did he ask for Aaron, or say anything about Moses?"

"No, he just called for you."

Jochebed slowly broke away from Miriam's embrace and, looking directly into her daughter's face, she said tenderly, "Thank you, little mama. I'll be all right now . . . you don't have to be my mother anymore . . . I think Jehovah is healing my heart."

"But Mother," Miriam countered, for she wasn't convinced that her mother was all right, "you mustn't live with the heavy regret of not being here when they brought father home. It couldn't be helped; the fever was so fast."

"Oh, my child." Jochebed faced the girl. "That's *not* the regret which troubles me so." Her voice was colored with sadness. "My strongest regret is that your father didn't live to see how Jehovah will deliver us from this evil land."

Aaron spoke up for the first time that night, and asked respectfully, so as not to offend her, "But, after all these years, do you still believe Jehovah will rescue us?"

Her son's words cracked like a whip across Jochebed's mind. Immediately she grabbed both Aaron's and Miriam's hands with conviction and whispered defiantly, "Listen! Jehovah *cannot* lie, my children. He *will* rescue us; and, furthermore, He will use you both . . . and especially Moses." Her voice softened and took on an ethereal quality. She mused, "Just think. Men like your father and you, Aaron, will not have to make the impossible bricks without straw. You and I," she glanced at Miriam, "will not have to work from sunup to sundown for the Egyptian dogs. And babies . . ." she grew wistful, "babies like Moses won't be thrown to the crocodiles. We will be delivered from our enemies. We *shall* leave Egypt . . . soon. You'll see."

Aaron acquiesced. He had to, for he could see his mother's old convictions had returned. She was stronger than ever in her hope-filled beliefs.

Jochebed refilled the small oil lamps and softly added, "Your father will not see the day . . . and maybe I won't either, but you children *will* leave Egypt as free people." Then, looking directly from son to daughter, she instructed, *"Believe* Jehovah. Someday He will use you to free the Israelites and to keep His promise to me . . . mark my words in your hearts."

It was the old familiar teaching, one that Aaron and Miriam had heard ever since Moses was born and went to live as a Prince and the son of Pharaoh's daughter. Both Miriam and Aaron believed their mother's dream would come true someday, but in the meantime life was beginning to take an exacting toll on the family of Amram. Deliverance, in reality, seemed only a small speck on the horizon of their daily existence.

A few weeks after their night-long talk with her mother, Miriam was startled to hear Jochebed say, "My daughter, if anything happens to me and I die before we are taken out of this land, will you do something for me?" The mother had only to ask, and she knew it, but she put it formally to Miriam so the girl would grasp the significance of her statement.

"Yes, Mother . . . what is it?"

"I want you to watch closely over Moses. See that the dream Jehovah gave me lives on in him. I want you to be his protector when he leads the people of Israel out, like you did when he was a baby at the river." Jochebed smiled as she remembered the fierce, mother-protector instinct her little girl had shown over the baby in the basket-boat.

"Haven't I always done just that?" Miriam smiled at her mother, and added, "I shall give it my full attention. In fact, I won't even marry, if it means giving up my 'Moses watch.' She was half joking, but only half, for her mother's training had duly soaked into the very fiber of her being; and, as when she was a child, the dream of being set free burned ardently within her, in spite of her doubts. As she looked at her mother and weighed her words, Miriam took a silent vow about her brother Moses. She would do her part now and in the future, in blind obedient faith, just as she had done earlier on the banks of the Nile. She gave up any hopes of marriage that day and prayed that Jehovah would bless her life with the kind of riches no husband could ever give. *It will be enough to take care of Prince Moses . . . more than enough,* she thought.

None of Jochebed's children ever forgot the instilling of truth their mother so deftly planted in their hearts.

But by the very next spring, just when all of nature—birds to flowers—was bursting forth with new life, a fever, not quite as quick as the one that took Amram, but just as lethal, came to the house of Jochebed. Before another seven days of spring had passed, the once vibrant life of this special woman slowly began to ebb away.

Weeks later, and just hours before Jochebed's death, Miriam hurried across the city to the palace and returned home with Moses. And there, with her children kneeling beside her pallet, the fevered woman looked lovingly into their faces and whispered, "I'm leaving you now . . . remember, *believe* Jehovah. Believe Him. Serve Him. . . . He will use you to lead us out of here. . . ."

She died without seeing how Jehovah would use her children, Aaron, Miriam, and particularly Moses, to lead the Hebrews out of Egypt. She died without seeing her faith and trust in Jehovah confirmed, and without seeing her greatest dreams come true.

But Jochebed died believing God.

PART III

Rahab

She was only close to being pretty, and a little too thin by the current beauty standards of Jericho's citizens, but everyone who knew Rahab rarely noticed her appearance.

Even when she was little, people were always taken by her bright, perky spirit. As girls went, she was sensitive and intuitive but much more boisterous than most. In fact, her brothers always thought of her as one of them. And by the time she reached her eighth summer she could fire off one stone from her sling shot, hit a tree a good distance away, and do it faster than the best of her brothers or their friends.

"She is rare, that one!" her father, Simri, had exclaimed on numerous occasions as she was growing up. "But by the gods, Reumah, why does she pester me with so many questions?"

Simri's wife went on weaving the flax on her small loom, and with a tiny smile playing around her mouth, she answered, "The child just *thinks* that way. What has she asked about now?"

"Chemosh." Simri shook his head. "She wants to know if it's true that only *girls* are offered as food to the god Chemosh. Where does one so young hear about our Amorite gods?"

Reumah stopped her weaving, and with a light chuckle replied, "My guess is, she asked too many questions of her brothers, and one of them told her that if she didn't stop it he'd feed her to the god Chemosh. He probably also scared her to death by adding that the only thing Chemosh eats is little girls."

Simri's short "Aha!" told her that he agreed. The subject of Chemosh had undoubtedly come up that way; but he added emphatically, slamming one of his fists into his open palm, "I tell you, woman, I'm not about to discuss Chemosh, Milcom, or Baal with anyone, much less a daughter!"

The truth was that Simri had very little working knowledge about the actual rites and practices of all the gods worshiped in Canaan. He did know that children were sacrificed alive to Chemosh; he had heard some of the brutal stories about the magic rites of Ashtoreth; and he knew, as did all the men who sat within Jericho's gates, that the mother goddesses of fertility who lived in the temple compounds were called "holy whores." But beyond that Simri neither knew much more, nor cared to learn. He was a simple man who minded his own business—drying flax and making products from it such as ropes and the linen cloths Reumah wove for him. His work, his men friends, and his sons were enough.

Reumah resumed her weaving. And as she moved the shuttle back and forth across the loom, she thought, *It's true, Rahab is always asking questions. That's just her way. She's curious about everything; she always wants to know all there is to know. She seems to be searching for truth. I don't like it. It's not becoming to a woman to think so much. Perhaps had she been born a man, life would have been easier for her.* Reumah had no trouble loving her unpredictable Rahab, but she rarely understood her—the only daughter among four sons.

A few months later Rahab went from her thirteenth year into her fourteenth, and on that same winter day, Simri rushed excitedly into the courtyard of their home fairly bursting with some incredible news. He'd spent the morning talking with his friends in the marketplace near one of Jericho's massive city gates. Now he hurried over to Reumah as she was tending the fires for their noonday meal.

"Rahab," he whispered urgently, "has Rahab flowered into her womanhood yet?"

"Yes, for a year now," Reumah answered, her voice puzzled. "Why are you asking? . . . Has she had a marriage proposal?"

"Yes. Yes!" Simri was slapping his hands together as though he'd gambled on something and won. "And wait till you hear of the dowry that's to be paid for her!"

"Who?" she demanded. "Who wants to marry her?"

"It's all settled, Reumah." He ignored the question and gestured with his hands for her to be quiet. "Tomorrow we will negotiate the final agreements. It will work out well. You'll see."

"But *who?*"

Her husband looked away, and Reumah immediately became fearful. She left her cooking pots and went to Simri. Trembling now, she steadied herself and measuring her words asked once more, "The man. What is his name?"

He pushed a couple of stones around in the dust with his sandal for a few moments, and then fearing what she would say, he responded quietly, "Kenaz."

Her eyes flew open and held there, widened in surprise. "Kenaz? The old man, Kenaz? The innkeeper on the wall?"

Simri nodded.

"But . . . but he's so old! In fact he's too old to use any woman for his pleasure, so he'll work her to death at the inn. Rahab will be a slave, nothing more. We'll never see her again. This isn't right," Reumah sobbed.

Simri put his arm around her shaking shoulders. "Now, now. It won't be like that. Kenaz has often seen our Rahab. He likes her spirit. He'll be good to her; I know he'll treat her kindly. His very words were that she would 'warm his old bones.' "

"Ha!" Reumah spit out vehemently. "What about his

wife's bones? They are still warm in her grave. Is *he* so
cold that he needs our Rahab?" Then, before Simri could
respond, she blurted out, "Oh, now I know! It's the dowry,
isn't it? The money was too good to turn down, so you
took Kenaz's offer and sold our daughter! It's the money.
Only the *money* you care about!" With that she sat down
on the doorway steps, bent over, and wailed into the folds
of her dress as though she were in deep mourning.

The sounds of her shrieking brought neighbors to their
windows, and Rahab flying into the courtyard. Reumah
caught sight of her daughter and only cried louder. "It's
the end of the world. The gods are destroying us. Kenaz
is a filthy old man." The girl was dismayed. She'd never
seen her mother so upset.

Reumah ranted and raved on for hours and would not
be comforted. But her brooding fears about the innkeeper
went unheeded because within days of Simri's announce-
ment, the marriage was formally negotiated and arrangements made for quick civil proceedings.

Rahab spent the last days of her girlhood, as was her
bent to do, questioning and pumping her mother, father,
and brothers for information about the mysterious rites of
marriage. Nobody was very helpful. Between her brothers'
humorous but uneducated guesses, and her mother's,
"Don't worry about it—you'll be too busy cleaning floors
and serving food at the inn to ever reach Kenaz's bed,"
to her father's hastily wrapping his turban around his head
and bolting for the door every time she came near him,
Rahab learned little that would prepare her for marriage.
But in her eyes, the whole thing—moving away, marrying,
and living in a busy inn—was something of a lark—a care-
free adventure.

A month later the "adventure" began. The marriage of
Kenaz and Rahab was performed and consummated, and
it was nothing like she'd imagined. It was infinitely better!

The inn, made of sun-dried bricks, was built up against

the inner wall of Jericho and over the top of both the massive inner and outer walls. It was a veritable paradise to Rahab.

The place was a beehive of bustling activity. The inn was filled with men from other cities and from far distant lands. Some bantered back and forth in strange languages, while others with mysterious and secretive ways conversed in low tones. But all were intriguing to Rahab. Servant girls raced about serving food and joined the men's bantering in a noisy but friendly fashion. Others served behind the scenes, preparing food, cleaning utensils, or just trying to keep up with the continual demand for wine. No matter what the hour, there was always some kind of activity taking place at the inn.

But the thing that held Rahab spellbound was the incessant swirl of conversations as the guests talked and noisily consumed the hot, savory food of the inn. The travelers were full of stories, tales, rumors, and war news. They spouted gossip, harangued each other over religion and the gods, discussed kings and governmental politics, wove together exotic tales of people and places, and bragged atrociously about their latest love conquests. None of this was lost on the new bride, and Rahab never tired of drinking deeply from the heady cups of their experiences.

And Kenaz, she thought, *what a wonder he is! Mother was wrong about him.* Rahab laughed aloud. Far from being "too old," as Reumah had warned, Kenaz took his bride to his bed every night. He proved, most assuredly, that he was not only able to enjoy the multihued excitement of a young wife, but could contribute to their time together as well.

Rahab found her husband a rather gruff man when he was in the presence of others, but when he was alone with her—he mellowed into a kind and gentle man. And in his bed, he became a teacher. He taught this girl-woman all the ways he knew, or had ever heard of, to pleasure a man.

In short, he answered all her questions—even some she'd
never thought to ask.

In return for his respect, kindness, and teaching, Rahab
willingly gave Kenaz her whole self. Many times after they
had made love, she regaled him with stories of her family
life, of her brothers' antics. But now and then she'd invent
amusing, whimsical incidences out of her own imagination.
And because she saw so much of what went on around
her that others missed, she developed extraordinary story-
telling abilities. So, besides giving Kenaz her body, she gave
him her spirit as well. She put the gift of wonder and laughter back into the old man's soul. And once she jested, "If
this is what's known as 'warming one's bones,' then I love
it!"

Kenaz became husband, father, and brother—all rolled
into one to Rahab. And a happiness, like the first rays of
the morning's light, kissed both their lives.

In the brief span of a year, Rahab, now fifteen, had
stepped out of her warm and uncomplicated childhood to
take her first unsteady steps in the crooked streets of the
cold adult world of reality.

She passed from girl to bride, to wife, to widow, all in
what seemed to be a moment. Rahab had been a joyous
bride and a hardworking, young wife. Her curious mind

was contented and even enchanted with all the various aspects of marriage and living at the inn. Her father's choice of a husband had been a good one after all. But then, just as she was beginning to sense a real purpose to her life, it had all come to a sudden, grinding end. Now Rahab was a bewildered widow, experiencing the annihilating, hammer-like blows of bereavement.

They buried Kenaz the same day he died, as was the country's custom, but it was weeks before Rahab could work through the labyrinths of her hurting and dazed mind.

Miraculously the inn seemed to carry on with business as usual. Rooms were full each night and, thanks to loyal servants and a few old friends, the inn remained open and flourished as if guided by Kenaz's unseen hand.

The practical and logical side of Rahab's reasoning powers was able to break through her grief first, and slowly she began to take stock of what she had and what she would do.

Kenaz had no other family, but still Rahab was surprised and grateful to learn that he had made legal arrangements, in the event of his death, for her to be the sole owner of his establishment. Whether her husband had had a premonition of his death or not, she couldn't know for sure. But, only a few nights before he died, Kenaz showed her a carefully constructed hiding place in the stone wall of their private rooms. Carefully he pulled out a section of rock and produced a goat-skin pouch. Then, without saying anything, as if the very walls had ears, he gestured to her that the secret contents of this purse were hers.

Now Rahab remembered Kenaz's actions and the pouch. She took the bag from its hiding place and carefully undid its leather ties to see what surprises it held. Several gold and silver weights spilled out on the table before her, followed by a small, but, what she felt had to be, extremely valuable collection of jewels. She recognized purple amethysts, a white beryl stone, some deep blue sapphires, and one rather large, shimmering green emerald. Several gold earrings completed the hoard, and all of it glinted and sparkled by the dim light of her oil lamps. For a long time she sat staring at the jewels and was warmed by the financial peace of mind they brought her.

She calculated that she would use these treasures only if she were forced to. She'd use them only if it were necessary. They'd be her emergency fund. *It will be enough*, she reasoned to herself. *I'll be able to stay here and keep the inn operating if I can just remember all the things I've learned from Kenaz. But if I fail now, during the busy season, what will I do if these jewels are not enough? How long can I last and stay here if the rains come and merchants and foreign travelers stay home or at other inns? Oh dear, there are so many ifs.*

The next morning, assembling all the bravery she could find within her, Rahab took stock of what she *did* have. And with logic beyond her years, she mentally added up the merits of her situation. Kenaz's death had left her a legacy that included both tangible and intangible assets. She now owned a well-known inn for her home and livelihood, a small collection of jewels for protection against rainy days, and a veritable education in the art of pleasuring a man—an asset she was sure she'd never have to put into practice. *Well, at least I don't have to worry about going into prostitution, if I can just work hard enough to keep the inn going*, she thought confidently.

The city of Jericho was rampant with all kinds of prostitution. There were temple whores who practiced their art for the sake of the gods or in the name of the goddesses of fertility under the sacred acacia trees in the hills surrounding Jericho. And then there were the common prostitutes who worked out of inns or just solicited business in the streets on their own. Not until she was married did Rahab know *what* a prostitute did exactly—only that whatever it was made men happy and the women despised. A prostitute was a social outcast, and other women refused to speak or even to look at her. Well, Rahab knew that while the citizens of Jericho heartily condoned and accepted *prostitution* as a way of life, they held a *prostitute* in great disdain even to the point of ostracizing her as untouchable as a leper. Prostitution was one thing, *being* a prostitute was quite another matter.

Rahab shuddered inside as she tried to comprehend what would happen to her relationship with her family, and all other women, if she had to use her body as a means of saving the inn and her life. Stubbornly, she determined that she'd be clever enough to stay in business without resorting to *that.* She was warmed by the memory of her father's business with flax, and reasoned, *I do know something of flax. I can dry it, weave it, and even learn to dye it.*

But Rahab was not old enough, wise enough, or strong enough to overcome the onslaught of dreadful events.

Valiantly, for four years after Kenaz's death, Rahab struggled to keep things going. But the years took their toll on her, and slowly but surely she could feel the ground slipping out from under her. The once nebulous *ifs* of her life materialized—in fact, even bunched up—and became responsible for rearranging her future.

If she could have kept the loyal servants and workers at the inn, maybe things would have gone differently. But, one by one, they died or grew too feeble to work, so she was forced to replace them with others. New servants neither cared nor understood how to perform their tasks; and, of course, they felt little loyalty to their mistress. So, they stole both time and food from their inexperienced employer. Even when Rahab hired two of her brothers, she eventually ran way behind in paying their wages, and soon they left the inn to seek out other work.

If, at the same time, taxes hadn't been doubled by the city authorities and another inn had not been opened and run by a powerful, well-known citizen of Jericho, perhaps she could have survived. At least she would have kept the pouch of precious stones from emptying so rapidly.

And *if* she could have devoted more time to the drying of flax instead of tending to the endless details at the inn, perhaps the flax business would have flourished and provided the needed extra income. But none of these events worked to her advantage. So, these and other *ifs* appeared and began to make good their threat to dismantle the inn of Kenaz—brick by brick, stone by stone.

"I see no other alternative, no other choice is left for me," Rahab explained to her mother one afternoon in the courtyard of her old home. Reumah, happy at first to see her daughter, had now turned away and was busying herself with stoking the cooking fires. Keeping her head down, Reumah moved the burning twigs and the flat, hot stones into different positions under the bubbling pot of lentil soup.

"Mother, I *know* what you're thinking, but I'll lose the inn unless I do it."

The older woman continued to bend over the fire. But now she made a small moaning sound and her tears splashed down and danced over the hot stones. Still, she said nothing, nor looked up at her daughter.

Rahab knelt down on the ground beside Reumah, and putting her arms around the older woman's shoulders, she pleaded, "Mother, listen. Please look at me. I don't want to be a prostitute, but . . . Kenaz left me the inn. It's my home, and I've worked very, very hard to make it profitable. But everything's gone wrong. I've given myself to it for four years. And I won't have it taken away from me now.

"You know how impossible this has all become. And you also know I can't come back here. I'd just be another mouth to feed." Rahab paused momentarily as though thinking to herself, and added, "and, as to my chances of marrying again, I know that if I save the inn by being a prostitute, nobody will be eager and anxious to marry me, but I *have* to try to save my house."

Reumah's sharp response cut deeply into the heart of Rahab. "Do you know what my neighbors will think? They'll talk about me, and they'll brand me as the mother of a whore!"

Rahab had not been prepared for this from her mother. Others, yes; but not Reumah, and she grew furious with the realization.

"Is that all you care about? That your friends and neighbors will talk?" Rahab was on the verge of shouting. "Don't you see that I have to," she stumbled over the words, ". . . I *have* to offer my services to the men who stay at the inn. It's the only way I can survive. You act as if I'm asking you to be a prostitute with me! But I only want you to understand *why* I'm doing this. I . . ."

A resounding slap across Rahab's face stopped her words, and Reumah said with smoldering intensity, "You'd better leave. I don't want to speak to you *ever* again. Go. Now. Before your father comes home."

It was the end, a final good-by—no, more like a final dismissal. Rahab gasped, "But I'm your daughter . . . surely you can show me some mercy?"

Reumah, her eyes dark with a wild rage, spit out venomously, "I don't *have* a daughter . . . only four sons. Now, get out!"

Rahab ran all the way through the winding, narrow streets, past the empty stalls at the marketplace—and didn't stop running until she reached the rooftop of the inn. There by herself, amid the stocks of flax, she finally allowed herself to cry. Her body was racked with great, convulsing sobs. But, in the morning, with the sparrows' first twittering, she rose up a determined woman. Rahab had firmly decided. She had chosen what she would do, and why. The time for crying had ended, and the time for doing had begun.

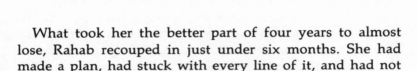

What took her the better part of four years to almost lose, Rahab recouped in just under six months. She had made a plan, had stuck with every line of it, and had not been the least surprised when it all succeeded.

Kenaz's inn on the wall became the talk of Jericho. Its reputation was quickly spread by merchant travelers from miles around. Once it was learned and verified that the vivacious innkeeper, Rahab, would sell her own body to the highest bidder, each and every night, men crowded into the inn. There was no end of customers, and the only problem at the inn was a continual shortage of rooms.

Wherever men congregated, whether privately or publicly, somewhere in their conversations the name of Rahab would come up and simply explode like a bright flash of lightning. Her outrageous originality was without doubt the subject of many discussions.

Aside from the unique idea of auctioning herself off each night, Rahab also determined that she'd give the highest bidder more than he bargained for. By using what Kenaz had taught her about the art of pleasuring a man, and adding another unrivaled gift of her own, Rahab was an instant success.

Her clients were astounded by her performance. In her own private room, she would delight and pleasure a man's body beyond his hopes or dreams. And then, to his joyance, she'd pleasure his spirit as well. She possessed an extraordinary ability to lift a man's heart to the heights of mirth and laughter by her uncommon, high-spirited gift for story-telling. She had known what this lifting of the spirits had meant to her husband Kenaz, so she drew on those memorable lessons.

Rahab's clients left her room knowing the price of the evening had been exorbitant, but believing it had been totally worth it. Both the man's body and his spirit had been immeasurably touched by her magic. There was hardly any way of keeping such an incomparable experience like that a secret. So Rahab's reputation circulated, like a light wind, over the city of Jericho.

The empty leather pouch was taken from its hiding place and began to swell with pieces of gold and silver and a growing number of fine stones. Rahab looked over the expanding collection and felt a deep satisfaction and sense of well-being about herself. *My ideas and persistence are paying off,* she thought proudly as she studied the enormous ruby glowing in her hand, *and I'm going to survive . . . on my own. I'll live!*

She was becoming more and more like Kenaz—an innkeeper who was tough, but fair, with the servants and hired hands. Those acquired traits, combined with her own inventive ideas, kept business at the inn booming. Just this afternoon, four men from the city council had met with her, given their blessing on her work, and had left assuring her of their interest and support. Rahab had smiled at their blessings and acceptance of her, for two of the authorities had been with her privately on other occasions and were already very supportive of her.

There were only two situations that withered Rahab's contentment. She was faced with the necessity of changing her daily routine and with accepting estrangement from her parents and brothers. One was easily remedied; the other, painfully formidable.

When Rahab had heard enough name-calling in the streets and at the marketplace, when she had endured all she could of the shunning of the women at the well, when she got tired of dodging stones thrown by small boys, and when she could no longer bear old women spitting at her, she changed her daytime patterns and habits. She accepted the fact that she was a prostitute and would be until she died. So she stayed indoors and simply assigned her hired girls the tasks of marketing, drawing the water, and handling the public errands. The changes in routine were quickly and efficiently worked out.

But bridging the huge chasm between her and her family proved to be about as easy as building one of those ancient tombs the merchants from Egypt were always arrogantly boasting about. After many failed attempts to contact and talk to Reumah or Simri, Rahab finally persuaded her youngest brother to come to the inn on a regular basis and give her a report regarding the family's health and whereabouts. Her suffering over the family rejection was the hardest part of being a harlot. And while she understood *why* she was untouchable, she still grew desperately lonely for their love, and mourned their loss.

Most of the time, operating the busy inn at full capacity, with days and nights consumed by arduous attention to detail, seemed to dull the ache in her soul over her parents and brothers. But as the months rolled on, and the immediate financial strain was lessened, Rahab—innkeeper and sole prostitute—pushed back her own personal hurts and began to really see and hear the world around her. Something of her old curiosity awakened in her, and soon she found herself asking questions of military men, travelers, merchants, foreign couriers, and local men, just as she had once done, as a child, with her father and brothers. Then her continual childish prattle and constant "whys" had driven her father wild. But now she was skillful in drawing out even the most reticent man, encouraging him to expound on what he had seen or heard in his travels.

Rahab learned how to filter out of her mind most of what was just rumor, gossip, or small talk from her guests at the inn. In this way, she kept an open channel in her mind and became adept at picking up on anything of a serious or important nature. She was blissfully happy when she was in the center of their conversations, debates, or discussions. The reports of news on wars and battles, the exotic stories told about kings and their far-off kingdoms, the merchants' wares she saw and touched—all of this made her feel as though the world were being brought to her, here in Jericho, since she couldn't go out to see it for herself.

But by far, of all the subjects discussed by the men, the matters involving Israel—its people, its leaders, and its God—fascinated Rahab the most.

Often she thought about these brave people with the strange customs; and, as her first successful year ended and she began another, she carefully pieced together the vast amount of information she had gathered on the Israelis.

Rahab remembered that they had been led by a man named Moses. Once, during a lively discussion between two Egyptian merchants, she had wondered aloud how the Israelis had found the courage to stand up to their Egyptian taskmasters and boldly leave Egypt. It was then that she first heard of their God—the one who had sent ten plagues to cripple the Egyptians. She wondered, *Did their God come down and personally fight their battles?* If so, He was quite remarkable. Then when Rahab was told about their forty years of wandering, she wondered what power kept them together. *Their God again?*

It seemed strange to Rahab that the Israelis had only one god while the people of Jericho had so many. *Wasn't it better, and certainly safer, to have more than one god? If you only had one god, what would you do if yours was sleeping, or he fumbled ineptly at answering your prayers?* Rahab sensed, as she listened to the men talk, that the God of Israel was highly unusual. She was *sure* of it when one of the men recounted the story of how Israel's God held back the Red Sea long enough to let them go across, but closed it up at the right moment just in time to swallow up the brutal Egyptians.

Now, the latest talk, especially from the travelers and merchants who came from the cities across the Jordan River, was rampant with incredible tales of Israel's new fearsome and invincible leader, Joshua. For some reason, the goose-flesh stood up on Rahab's arms the first night she heard Joshua's name. The men buzzed with admiration for Joshua, for it seemed that under his leadership Israel's army had been completely victorious in every war they waged. Rumors were widespread, but the one that made the most sense was that it would be just a matter of time before Joshua would work his way across the Jordan River from the east, and conquer Jericho. Just yesterday two different sources verified that Joshua and his army were camped at Shittam near the vast groves of acacia trees just across the river. *With him that close, will it be long before he moves against us?* the young innkeeper wondered.

Rahab, having lived all her life in the fortress city of Jericho, realized the importance of its exact location at the lower end of the Jordan valley. It was situated near the important roads and strategic mountain passes which led westward. And if it were true that this Joshua planned to rule the whole land of Canaan, then Rahab also knew it didn't take too much military insight to see that in order for Joshua to possess the great central division of Canaan, he would first have to destroy and conquer Jericho.

The more Rahab heard about Joshua, his fearless leadership and his conquests, the more inquisitive she became about his God. *How does one find this God? Where is His temple? What does He demand as sacrifices? Is He good or evil, mean or loving? Where does He live?* These and other questions filled her mind. She felt a great hungering within her, and every time she heard someone talking about this remarkable God she feasted at His unseen table; but left it unsatisfied and wanting more.

Since Israel's God knew she was seeking and searching

for Him, He called to her in a very strange way and on one of her busiest of nights.

Rahab was making her way through the noisy groups of men in the crowded main chamber of the inn, trying to get a small goatskin of wine to one of her customers, but she kept getting delayed. Everyone was eating, drinking, and in a boisterous mood! In the midst of this tumult created by men in high humor—content with their fill of food and wine—Rahab glanced toward the doorway. Instantly her body went rigid with the surprise of recognition.

No one else seemed to notice them, but for Rahab it was as though everyone—men and serving girls alike—disappeared in a flash and there were just she and the two young men in the doorway. And with equal intensity they had singled her out of the crowd and were solemnly staring at her.

They must be Israelis, she thought, wondering why she was so sure of that. *Either they are simple fools or extremely clever to come in here so brazenly and risk being recognized . . . or has their God sent them?* A chill, in spite of the hot, stuffy room ran down her back, and in an instant she knew what she would do.

Rahab turned and caught the eye of the man who wanted the wine she carried, and with a wink she tossed him the goatskin. He missed the flying goatskin, and it hit the wall and broke, spattering wine all over him. In the midst of the confusion and laughter which ensued, Rahab hurried to the men in the doorway.

The fierce, black eyes of the taller man bore into her soul, searing her greatly, but with an iron-willed composure she announced, "I'll give you shelter."

In view of the fact that her words were tantamount to treason, she was a little startled that she'd uttered them so deliberately and casually. The thought did skip across her mind that, should she be caught harboring these men, the king of Jericho would certainly show no leniency or mercy. Yet, as she figured it, one way or another—by Jericho's king or Israel's army—she was probably going to die anyway. And if she were given a choice, she didn't know why, but she preferred to be at the mercy of the Israelis.

So, Rahab passed between the two men, out the doorway, and walked quickly into the street, issuing the order, "Come!" as she moved away. In blind trust and silent obedience, the two men followed her around the corner of the inn and up a narrow outside staircase to the roof.

In the dusk of the early evening, there was just enough light for them to see that one side of the roof was covered with flax which had been laid out to dry. Rahab lifted several stocks of the long, tapered-leafed plants and said, "Lie down here, and I'll cover you with this." No response was needed from the men because they had each decided to entrust their welfare to her keeping. "I'll be missed if I don't get back, but take your rest here and later, when I can, I'll bring you some food. Don't worry, I'll come back." She hurriedly gave them two flat cushions for their heads and arranged several stocks of flax over them.

Rahab never discovered who informed the authorities that night of the arrival of the two men, but soon after she resumed her duties and began mingling with her guests, a small army of men sent by the king appeared at the inn. They demanded that Rahab surrender the two spies into their custody.

The officer towered over the diminutive innkeeper as he shouted, "We know they are here; now get them! They are spies sent by the Israeli leaders to find the best way to attack us, and we want them."

It was as though she'd waited her whole life for this one exciting moment. She fairly tingled all over with the sheer love of the unfolding drama. Making her eyes very wide with untarnished innocence, Rahab explained breathlessly, "You're right! They were here, but I had no idea they were spies."

"Where are they now?" the officer barked.

"Oh, they left the city at dusk, just as the eastern gates

were about to close. I don't know where they went after that." She was doing so well with her guileless performance that she added the suggestion, "If you hurry, you can probably catch up with them." Later she heard that on the basis of her suggestion, the officer and his men pursued the elusive spies all the way to the Jordan River.

It was very late before she could successfully manage to leave her responsibilities as innkeeper and the client who was the high bidder for the evening; but when she did, Rahab returned with bread, cheese, and wine for the secluded guests on the rooftop.

She sat on the floor beside them as they eagerly devoured all she'd brought, and then watched as they leaned back against the bundles of flax.

"My name is Rahab," she whispered.

"I am Salmon." The tall man with the piercing eyes spoke.

"Joab," murmured the younger man.

"I hid you tonight and lied for you when the king's men came looking for you because I *know without a doubt* that your God is going to give my country to you.

"We are all afraid of you," Rahab continued. "In fact, everyone is terrified if the word *Israel* is even mentioned. For a long time now, we have heard about your reputation. We heard about the time your God made a path through the Red Sea for you when your people left Egypt with Moses. And we know what you did to Sihon and Og, the Amorite kings who lived east of the Jordan, and how you ruined their land and completely destroyed their people. It's no wonder we are so afraid of you!"

Both men exchanged glances, and Rahab saw their slight smiles by the tiny flickerings of her oil lamp.

"You must know, Salmon, no one has any fight left in him after hearing things like that, for your God is the supreme God of all gods in heaven and in earth. He is not just an ordinary god." She marveled at her own words, for she *knew* what she said was completely true.

Rahab felt a great longing to personally know the God

of these men, and so in those moments she decided to put herself at their mercy. She pleaded, "Now I beg for this one thing: Swear to me, by the sacred name of your God, that when Jericho is conquered you will let me live, along with my parents, my brothers, my sisters-in-law, and all their families."

The men remained silent, so Rahab added, "This is only fair, after the way I've protected you tonight."

Without any discussion, the men agreed, and aloud Salmon promised, "If you won't betray us, we'll see to it that you and your family aren't harmed. We'll defend you with our lives."

Rahab breathed a sigh of relief, not only because she *knew* instinctively they'd keep their word, but because leaving Jericho after it was conquered was the only way of gaining back her family. She'd be through with the inn; she was wealthy with more than enough money; and, best of all, she'd be through with whoring. The hope of being restored to her parents and the whole family brought a surge of excitement through her soul.

In the darkest part of the night, when the spies felt the safest, Rahab found her longest rope. She had been learning dyeing techniques and she'd dyed the coarse flax fibers of this rope a bright crimson red.

"Come with me to a room downstairs. I'll help you out the window and let you down the outside wall with this rope." Again they silently followed her. Rahab secured the rope to one of the ceiling beams. As they were climbing out the window, she instructed, "Escape to the mountains. It would be best for you to hide there for at least three days until the men who are searching for you have returned. Then go your way."

Salmon stood thoughtfully fingering the bright strands of the scarlet rope, and looking directly down at her said, "Rahab when we do return to Jericho, we cannot be responsible for what happens to you unless this rope is hanging from this window and unless all your relatives—your father, mother, brothers, and anyone else—are here . . . inside this house."

Rahab nodded.

"If they go out into the street, we assume no responsibility whatsoever; but, we *swear* that no one inside the inn will be killed or injured." Then Salmon threatened, "However, if you betray us, then this oath will no longer bind us in any way."

"I agree . . . I accept your terms."

They left even more quickly than they had appeared. And long after they were gone, Rahab still stood clutching the rope she'd left hanging down Jericho's outside wall.

Morning's light found her there, still astonished by the events, the strange but wonderful events, that had taken place. Rahab began making her plans. She would convince her parents and family to come to the inn when Joshua and the Israeli army began their seige. *How,* she did not know, but convince them, she would. She was sure of that, and of one other thing: the God of Israel would be her God . . . her *only* God.

The people of Jericho sensed that an incredible war would be waged on their large and heavily fortified city. Daily, from behind their impregnable double walls and tightly sealed gates, they waited and watched. Everyone—from little children to the king and all his men—duly recorded in their minds the preposterous antics of Joshua's army. No one fathomed or believed what they saw. It was unlike any other military battle or maneuver they'd ever heard of or observed.

For six days Israel's army took a ludicrous walk around the entire city of Jericho. Almost everyone in the city had a theory, explanation, or opinion as to what Joshua was doing, but the most prevailing and common rationale centered on the Israeli religion.

It was rumored and fervently hoped that this daily march was merely some sort of harmless pre-battle requirement to appease their God. This conclusion was predictable because when the Israelis walked around their city each day, Joshua and his officers led the procession, and they were followed by the main body of the army. Seven men, dressed in what appeared to be the robes of priests, came next, carrying long rams' horns, presumably trumpets. And finally, bringing up the rear, were more priests, shouldering what looked like a religious relic—an oblong chest that was rumored to be Israel's holy ark. Even the king subscribed to this idea. And it gave him a measure of hope, for he felt that when Joshua had fulfilled his God's idiotic requirements and actually began the battle—the warriors of Jericho would then stand a fighting chance of winning.

Only Rahab, who watched and waited just like all the others, was of a completely different persuasion. From the moment she'd seen Salmon and Joab in the doorway of the inn, the night she hid them, there had begun to grow an invincible *knowing* within her. It was not as though she were a fortuneteller or suddenly had the ability to prophesy, but rather the serene assurance that sight unseen, Israel's God was real. Without understanding her feelings, an ardent trust in this God began pumping strangely through Rahab's veins. And, to her surprise, each new day the Israeli God revealed Himself to her in an unexpected way; so she grew even stronger in her new-found beliefs and trust.

She also became stubbornly confident that this God, and *only* this God, was the true, the *living* God. Joining Salmon, Joab, and the people of Israel—to serve this God became the driving force and ambition of her life. And just as Rahab had worked and schemed to keep from losing the inn after Kenaz's death, now she fought equally hard to leave it. But she was determined to take her family with her.

From that first significant meeting with the Israeli spies, Rahab had thought not only of saving herself, but of the deliverance of her whole family as well. However, it had been a few years now, almost four, since she'd become a harlot; and all contact with her family was broken, save for an occasional report from her brother. Her fears assailed her. *What if my father will not listen to me? What if he listens, but will not believe me when I tell the family that the Israeli God will, indeed, win the war? If I fail to convince them to come and stay here at the inn, they will die . . . all of them. I know the Israeli God and Joshua's men are about to rain death and destruction down on everyone here in Jericho!* she thought as panic rose within her.

The first day of Joshua's march around the city's walls, Rahab could see that it would be only a short time before the end would come. The battle would begin and end in a twinkling of an eye. She felt the invisible urging of the Israeli God, and she *knew* the time had come to go to her family, to convince and alert them about the terrifying power of this God. So, with brazen courage and blunt honesty, Rahab waved aside Reumah and Simri's objections to her presence, and stormed like a whirlwind into her parents' house.

"I must speak my piece to you. And when I've finished, I'll leave, but please, just hear me out." Carefully she chose her words in order to capture their attention, yet still not showing disrespect for them.

Deliberately refusing to look at his daughter, Simri stared past Rahab to the wall; and Reumah averted her eyes as though, by looking, she'd be contaminated by her daughter's unholy disease. Two of her brothers stood silently by the back wall.

Undaunted by their rejection and their horror at her *being* in their house, Rahab continued. "You know I have never been interested in the gods we have . . . I'm not a religious person. But, in the last few years, I have heard stories and tales of the remarkable Israelis and their powerful God. I've personally met with two Israelis, and my heart has told me two things."

Now both her mother and her father were staring at Rahab. "Go on," Simri urged, surprising himself.

"Well . . . ," Rahab paused and gulped a deep breath of air. "I know the Israeli God will help Joshua and his army to completely destroy us. *Everyone* will die. No one will escape the wrath of this God. He is not *anything* like Jericho's gods."

Reumah's face turned gray and one of her hands flew to her mouth, while the other grabbed Simri's arm.

"Everyone?" Simri asked in a stricken voice.

"Yes. *Everyone* will die," she shouted in the agony of her desperation. "The other thing my heart *knows* for certain is that there is a way of escape for all of us, but *only* if you do exactly as I say. You'll have to trust me," she pleaded "and you'll have to come with me."

For a moment the silence was deafening, and then Simri gave his solemn pronouncement, "We will. We'll do whatever you want."

"There is very little time." Rahab's voice was steady and calm. But her father's response made her tremble with a joyous relief, and while she showed her family an iron front, full of strength and confidence, she was glad her skirt hid the violent knocking of her knees.

It took the better part of the afternoon and all that evening to move the whole family into the inn. Rahab arranged and rearranged each and every detail. She assisted her parents, her brothers, her two sisters-in-law, and their babies with the intricate job of moving and settling in. The family understood they would stay there with Rahab for the duration of the siege. She left no detail undone. After she was satisfied that the family was comfortably situated, she went to the cooking quarters and paid her servants and hired hands their wages, tearfully sending them home. Then, resolving to be undaunted by the impending doom, she courageously shut and barred the inn's main door for the last and final time.

The scarlet rope of flax hung down the outer wall as a flag to mark their peaceful intentions and their whereabouts. Each morning the whole family gathered on the top of the wall to watch the great army of Israel keeping their strange marching vigil.

It was still dark, just before dawn on the seventh day of Joshua's marching, when Rahab was awakened by the cry of one of the infants in the room adjoining hers. She lay awake listening to her brother's wife hushing the baby, when suddenly she *knew* this was the day. Hurriedly, she dressed and rushed up the stairs to the roof. It was still too dark to see anything, so she sat down to wait on the low stone edging of the roof's outer wall.

Presently, in the darkness, Rahab was aware that someone else had joined her. She rose to meet whoever it was, and then froze as she heard the softly spoken greeting, "My daughter."

Rahab and Reumah fell into each other's arms. Wordlessly they clung together in a fierce embrace and wept. Neither mother nor daughter apologized, explained, or spoke; but, both women understood the chasm between them was now bridged. The past was gone, the future unpredictable; and since the present was all they really had, they dried each other's tears and soundlessly agreed to begin afresh.

With the first lavender-gray light of morning, Rahab and Reumah looked down at the endless line of men. For as far as they could see, in both directions, the city of Jericho was surrounded by Joshua's vast army. Marching in silent cadence, the soldiers had filed into place and formed a human chain around the city. Then, as mother and daughter watched, by some invisible signal, the men began their familiar march around the city.

Much later, one of Rahab's brothers shouted down the stairs, "They are going around again. I can see Joshua right now rounding the corner!" Rahab was preparing food in the cooking area, and without stopping she called up, "How many times has that made now?"

"Four! They've gone around four times. What does it mean?" her brother called down to her.

Rahab was convinced now that the departure from Joshua's usual once-around-the-city was a significant change. She left the heat of the cooking fires and hurried to the roof. "I think all the extra marching is proof that *today* Jericho will fall to Joshua." And then to give the small family band courage, Rahab patted her father's arm and said, "Jericho will be destroyed, but *we'll* be delivered . . . you'll see."

They ate their noonday meal up on the roof—the whole family, babies and all.

"They are on their seventh time around," Simri announced. The words had barely left his mouth when all of them were startled by a loud, eerie sound which split the air, hurt their ears, and made the babies cry all at once.

"It's the priests! They're blowing those ram horns!" someone yelled. Then a new tumult began. All the armed soldiers in Joshua's army gave up a great shout, sending up an alarming, earsplitting noise.

The trumpets, the men shouting, and the unseen hand of the Israeli God began to shake Jericho as though it were a limp rag doll. Stone after stone in the massive walls moved, pitched, and tumbled loose from its place with a booming roar.

Rahab and her family fled the roof and came down to huddle together in the main room of the inn. They were panic stricken by the terrifying crescendo of noise around

them. But steadying herself as much as possible Rahab un-
barred the door. Then they waited for the Israeli soldiers
and the deliverance that Rahab *knew* would come.

The army of Israel was now ravaging about in the city
streets, for the "impregnable" walls—with the exception
of the inn's wall—were no longer standing. Joshua's instructions were simple and final: destroy everything that moves
and everything that stands still. Nothing was to be left of
men, women, children, oxen, sheep, donkeys, houses, or
market stalls. Everything was to be destroyed.

From the part of the wall that was still standing the Israeli
soldiers could easily see the scarlet rope hanging against
the sand-colored stone. And as they rushed to the inner
side Rahab threw open the inn's door. Her heart broke
into undisguised joy when she easily recognized the tall
stature and the piercing brown eyes of the first soldier she
saw.

"Salmon!" she cried.

"Yes." The big man smiled down at her, and then he
yelled above the battle din, "Is all your family here?"

Rahab nodded her head quickly.

"Then, come on. Let's go. We'll get you out of the city."
And gesturing up to the floor above them, he cautioned.
"Your part of the wall is going to come down any moment
now, so we'd better move quickly and get out of here!"

Rahab and Salmon were the last to hurriedly leave the
inn. Behind her was her old way of life; and now, out
there in the Israeli encampment, a strange new life awaited
her. She calmed her fearful anticipation by fingering the
bulge of precious stones tucked beneath her dress sash.
*When we reach the camp, I'll give it all to the Israeli God who saved
us today,* she promised herself as she fled the destruction
behind her.

Salmon helped her carry several bundles of household
goods and clothing as they picked their way through the
giant mounds of stone and rubble. When they cleared the
last enormous pile of rocks and reached the first clearing,

Rahab fell into an exhausted heap; yet, somehow her spirit was exhilarated and soaring like an eagle who has just been freed from his cage. She was free, her family was free. They were delivered.

Just as she was about to express her gratitude to Salmon, they heard a thunderous rumbling and grinding noise behind them. They turned their heads in time to see the wall and what had been her home crumble into a million pieces. Right before the brown cloud of smoke and dust obscured their vision, both Rahab and Salmon saw a streak of red amidst the stones as it flashed in the sunlight.

When the dust settled, Rahab turned to speak her thanks to Salmon, but when she saw his face she asked, "Why are you looking at me like that?"

"I . . . it was nothing." He helped her up.

"But, I want to know . . . what were you thinking?"

Salmon's face reddened with a touch of embarrassment, but he replied, "I was just remembering. This morning Joshua called Joab and me to his headquarters and ordered, 'Keep your promise. Go and rescue the prostitute and everyone with her,' and . . ."

"And what?"

"It's just that you don't *look* like a prostitute."

Rahab smiled. "I'm not, now."

And, with a toss of her head, she began walking resolutely and a bit triumphantly toward the Israeli tents and her waiting family. She felt a quiver of excitement run down her back as she wondered what serving the Israeli God would really mean. She could feel nothing but hope and expectant joy about the life that lay in front of her.

As she reached the tents, she turned and looked at Salmon coming toward her and thought, *Someday, Salmon,· I'm going to marry you.*

Rahab just *knew* it.

PART IV

Abigail

"David replied to Abigail, 'Bless
the Lord God of Israel who has
sent you to meet me today!'"

1 Samuel 25:32

She was supervising her servant women as they served the festive evening meal, when one of her husband's guests verified what up to now had been only a dark rumor.

So it's true! Abigail thought. A wave of uncertainty washed over her, but she carried on as though she'd not heard. For the last week there had been rumors and fragmented stories, but none of the people of Carmel really knew for sure. Until now. But now she knew it was true—the prophet and judge, Samuel, or the "great seer" as he was commonly called by the people of Israel, was dead and buried.

The three men who were guests at Nabal's table were wool merchants from the north, all of whom had come directly from Samuel's funeral in Ramah. They sat on rugs in the most spacious tent of their host Nabal, eagerly devouring Abigail's meal of well-roasted lamb, but their conversation did not concern itself with the business of buying Nabal's wool. Instead, they talked of Judah's precarious future, now that Samuel was dead.

And with cautious respect, they questioned how King Saul would rule now . . . without Samuel's godly wisdom.

Intuitively, Abigail knew that Samuel's death darkened Israel's future considerably. She, along with every son of

Jacob, whether he was a farmer, rancher, or merchant, understood that the political ramifications of this man's death were enormous.

Soon even the people who lived in the outlying provinces and wilderness parts would hear the news of Samuel's death, and Nabal's guests talked of how the mourning for the seer would soon be evident throughout the entire land. They speculated further that even those who felt that Samuel was somewhat enigmatic knew that he had been a man you could trust and believe.

"What iron flowed in his veins," praised Abner, one of the merchants. "Remember how he stood up to anyone when Jehovah told him to . . . even to King Saul?" The others, including Nabal—who rarely said yes on any occasion—nodded their agreement.

"Such a man! And even with all that power he remained incorruptible. Yes, there was a man you could trust. But who will replace him?" Abner wondered as he sopped his bread into the lamb juices.

"Well," injected Jeiel, "even if you didn't like the seer or you disagreed with his pronouncements, there wasn't a man alive who would have openly disputed his authority. Clearly, Samuel had both ears of Jehovah!" The others listened to the little man, not because he was the most wealthy of the merchants, but because he had been born and raised in Ramah, Samuel's home town. And this gave him a special air of credibility.

As she listened to the men's talk, Abigail recalled that for many years the people of Israel had repeatedly experienced the terrible oppression of the Philistines. They had indeed come to believe that Jehovah had abandoned them to their fate. But it had been Samuel who put his finger squarely on the real problem. With bold righteousness he came before the people and said that if they were *really* serious about wanting Jehovah in their midst and returning to Him, then they'd have to get rid of all their foreign gods and Ashtaroth idols and obey *only* Jehovah.

Always attentive to her guests, Abigail now replaced an empty tray with one heaped with sheets of thin, crusty bread and smiled to herself as she remembered how the people took Samuel's words to heart. The Hebrews had done as Samuel instructed and their obedience to the seer's words of warning had put the first major crack in the walls of Philistine domination over them.

Nabal and his guests continued to reminisce about Samuel's character and his lifetime of carrying out Jehovah's instructions. Their conversation lasted long into the night after they had eaten their fill of honey raisin cakes and had consumed many skins of wine.

Abigail, though she came into the tent as often as it seemed reasonable and stayed as close as she dared, had many questions, but she knew better than to ask. She hoped that going in and out of the tent and efficiently seeing to her husband and his guests' pleasures would help her to glean all the information she so eagerly sought.

Their cultural mores did not consider it proper for a woman to have an unsolicited conversation with a male guest unless she was invited to do so by her husband. In Abigail's case, her husband, Nabal, had never allowed her to converse much with him much less with other men. Early on in their prearranged marriage, Abigail had used all her skills in trying to draw Nabal out in conversation, but it soon proved to be a hopeless task.

"Woman," he had sneered one day, "let it be enough for you that some men *say* you are beautiful. But, beautiful or not, you are my wife, and I want you to keep your thoughts to yourself. Don't clutter the air in my tents by clucking like a hen."

In the interest of maintaining any semblance of peace, Abigail soon learned to respond to Nabal's rudeness with obedient silence. Quickly she caught on to the truth that her silence and a sense of timing were her only allies in making her marriage bearable at all.

Privately, locked in the closed-off rooms of her heart

and mind, Abigail knew her husband was, as his name implied, an ill-mannered, churlish fool. Yes, he was the richest rancher in the whole country south of Jerusalem, and he was shrewd when it came to the business of sheep and goats, but he was still a fool.

Even from the first days of her marriage when she was barely sixteen, Abigail had understood that this marriage, arranged by her father and uncle, was certainly not going to be easy. But she kept her true feelings to herself most of the time. Now and then, though, because of disputes or unpleasant circumstances, she was forced to deal with or speak to the blunt reality of her husband's offensive nature. To her everlasting credit, however, she remained loyal to Nabal and steadfastly endeavored to be the only agent of reconciliation in the marriage.

Actually, Nabal was much better in understanding the ways of his flocks and herds than of the people around him. And he was especially blind when it came to his wife.

Everyone in the town of Carmel and in the surrounding mountainous country of Judah, who knew the wealthy but cantankerous rancher and his beautiful, well-spoken wife, talked and gossiped about the obvious injustice their union provoked. But if the men in the community were politely guarded in their conversations and dealings with Nabal because they feared his sudden bursts of wrath, they were simultaneously pleased beyond belief to be a guest in Nabal's tents—partly because they were all smitten with the breathtaking beauty of Abigail and partly because of Nabal's wealth.

The villagers, shepherds, hired servants—men and women alike—often said the wife of Nabal was like a refreshing, fragrant spring bouquet. It was said too, that her beauty, like honeysuckle blossoms, gentled the roughness of the people and seemed to temper the harsh wildness of the country. But it was Abigail's words which outshone her beauty for they were well thought out and scented with wisdom.

Not only was Abigail's beauty ignored by Nabal, but

her brightness of mind and spirit as well. It escaped his attention that Jehovah had matched, as it were, her face and form with an equally exquisite mind. Abigail's keen intelligence chased and caught ideas and information faster than many a wise-thinking man.

Carmel's gossip had it that Nabal rightly knew and understood his wife's unique abilities. But his blind, rebellious heart, paralyzed with envy and jealousy, refused to acknowledge either Abigail's beauty or intelligence. Some believed that it was Nabal's drinking which crippled his mind and heart, but those who worked with him said that it made no difference, for even when he was cold sober he made crude jests and ill-mannered remarks about his wife and about women in general.

"They are like our prime ewes and strong she-goats," Nabal boasted. *"Best* for breeding!" Then he'd laugh, forgetting that he and Abigail were childless, and failing to notice that few of the men agreed with or saw any humor in his crudeness.

"Our mistress, Abigail, is amazing!" her servant girls heartily conceded. "Even though our stupid master has shut her out of his heart and thoughts, she refuses to become bitter or take her anger out on us!" Abigail smiled as she overheard her servants talking, and to herself she thought, *Nabal was chosen to be my husband for better or worse. I would have died early in this marriage from the wounds of his words and actions, but Jehovah has sustained me. He has made me quietly strong through this union, and He has increased my ability to endure.*

Often during the years of the marriage to Nabal, Abigail used the lessons of suffering to comfort the hurting hearts around her, and each time Jehovah blessed her efforts. Her character grew stronger because of the never-ending conflicts. And, strangely enough, her face too grew more beautiful.

Tonight, here in Nabal's main tent, however, Abigail's sense of timing and gracious silence were severely tested. The presence of the wool merchants provided an excellent opportunity to hear news of the outside world, and her thirst for information was nearly unquenchable. She grew increasingly impatient. Abigail watched and waited for her chance. Then, once she assessed Nabal's mind to be sufficiently dulled by the wine, she poured more wine into Jeiel's cup and whispered, "What do the people say of David ben Jesse now that the seer is gone?"

The question fell on the ears of the merchants exactly as she intended. Up to this point they had not talked of Samuel's annointed king-elect, David. But Abigail suspected that each of them had privately wondered whether or not King Saul would continue his vendetta and try to kill David.

Jeiel, flattered to the point of blushing, was thrilled that the beautiful Abigail had asked such an important question of him and was inordinately pleased to expound on David. For he, like his friends, put all Israel's hope in the great David ben Jesse.

Without looking in Abigail's direction, but for her benefit, Jeiel said, "Who of us can fathom what will happen to David now?" Then, dropping his voice, he grew confidential. "No one *knows* what the mind of King Saul holds." He then hinted at the black rumors which circulated frequently around the country concerning Saul's apparent fits of depression and madness. "But I, for one," Jeiel continued, "am sure that David, our warrior-hero, is more than a troublesome burr under the King's saddle. He is definitely the throne's most flagrant threat."

The men, with the exception of Nabal who was now fast asleep, murmured their agreement. Their beloved nation, strewn about like broken pieces of pottery, had lost the only godly leader they'd ever known. Now these men longed desperately for a man to lead and heal their people and unite their fragmented nation.

Abner motioned for Abigail to sit with them. Because her curiosity was not nearly satisfied, she eagerly and gratefully accepted the offer. And as she tucked her skirts under her she asked softly, "Did David return to Ramah for Samuel's burial?"

"No," answered Eliab, the most quiet of the three. The woman's presence and beauty warmed his spirit while loosening his reticence to speak. "It would have been too risky for David; he might have lost his head had he made the journey."

"Ah, then David and his men are still here with us in these mountains?" Abigail asked, then added, "Did you know that out of the goodness of his soul David and his band of men have guarded our herds and flocks for some time now?" She asked the question only to inform them, since the safety of the wool from these herds was of vital interest to the men. From the obvious pride in her voice, they guessed her loyalty was not to King Saul, but to king-elect David. The question freed them to openly talk of their hopes for Israel with David, not Saul, as their king.

"If I were David, and of course I'm not . . . but if I were," Abner pondered aloud, "I'd take my men to Saul's home in Gibeah, kill him and every mother's son in his army, and take my rightful place as king! After all, David was anointed by Samuel when he was just a lad. Now it's time."

"I agree, Abner," said Eliab, "in that David is Israel's hope. But what can he do with only five or at the most, six hundred men against Saul's thousands? Besides, if Saul ever caught a whisper of David's plans, he'd call out the fighting men from every city and village in the country, and every man and boy of us would have to march against David . . . oh, the odds." Eliab pulled on his full, white beard and solemnly shook his head.

"David didn't have any men with him when he killed Goliath," Abigail interjected quietly. The men's faces brightened considerably.

"True . . . true," whispered Jeiel with conviction. "And wouldn't I have liked to have been there to see it! Can you picture Goliath's face as David shouted up, 'You come to me with a sword and a spear, but I come to you in the name of the Lord of Hosts, the God of the Armies of Israel'?"

Abigail's eyes flashed with her mind's imaginative paintings of that triumphal day.

For a moment the group sat stilled and thoughtful as they each mused about the incredible young shepherd boy who had brought down the giant Philistine with one name and one stone.

"I think . . ." Abigail said, breaking their reverie, "David is the only man alive, chosen by Jehovah, who could unify the disorganized tribes of Israel. He is our hope, our *only* hope to lead our nation into greatness and glory."

The merchants, agreeing with the truth of her words, nodded their heads in awesome respect for her political assessments.

Abigail loved being included in their conversation, and it was obvious that the men liked it too because their huddled talk went on until the first violet-gray light of dawn came over the eastern hills.

In the days that followed her conversation with the merchants from the north, Abigail had little time to reflect or ponder the fate of David, the king-elect.

Of utmost priority, in Abigail's mind, was the preparation

of food for the festivities that come with shearing time. She was involved with the dressing and roasting of lambs, the baking of bread, and then the serving of it all to the men on their ranch. Spring was on the wane, and they were well into May. It looked now as if they would be finished with the washing and shearing of sheep by the middle or end of June. These were days of hard work and light-hearted merriment, and Abigail's responsibility was to provide enjoyment for the men at sunset with bountiful banquets of food and drink. Her days compared well to those of the farmers' wives at the autumn harvest of crops. There were two months of continuous labor, morning and evening meals, and the unmistakable jesting and camaraderie amongst the men. The workers—shepherds and hired hands—formed kindred spirits with each other, as it often happens among men who share a common purpose, work hard, and are a part of a smoothly-run working team.

Approximately three thousand sheep and one thousand goats belonging to Nabal had been rounded up and herded in from the hillsides and valleys around Carmel. And some of the men and dusty flocks had come in from the distant Paran wilderness which stretched along the edges of the Sinai desert. Hired hands and shepherds alike, tired, but glad to be home, washed and sheared sheep during the day, and ate and drank their weight and sang festive songs through much of the night.

Abigail, up a few hours before dawn and rarely retiring until all were settled, was both exhausted and exhilarated. She always looked forward to these months of late spring before the summer sun burned the green from the valleys for they culminated a whole year's worth of work. Their vast lands had never been more beautiful, set in the lush green valleys, and their healthy flocks and herds had never been more prolific. Mostly though, Abigail loved the shearing season because it provided a breathing space from Nabal. Her husband, involved either with the shearing supervision or indulging in his wineskins, left Abigail to the enormous domestic tasks. Gratefully, she accepted these days and the relief they provided from the harsh realities of Nabal's harassment and rejection.

Nabal, even on his better days, was an extremely difficult man to deal with. But, now, during the ribaldry of the festivities—with all the increased amounts of wine he was putting away—the man was *beyond* difficult. Way beyond. His churlish disposition soured even more and his already warped sense of humor degenerated into biting sarcasm with each day the sheep-shearing continued.

Abigail knew beyond any shadow of doubt that it was to Nathaniel's credit that the mood among the men was good and the work ran smoothly. Nathaniel, a short, stocky man, was chief overseer of the ranch. Gifted with stoic patience and an iron will, he managed to hold his ground with the master; and, in a curious way, Nabal had kept his distance and even showed the foreman some semblance of respect. However, the one thing Nathaniel did not do with Nabal was talk.

The overseer was, by nature, a hoarder of words, but it was especially true when he was with Nabal. There he confined himself to occasional eye contact, brief nods, and low, guttural sounds. The verbal expressions of his heart and mind were locked away *unless* he was with Abigail.

When Nathaniel was in her presence the floodgates of his inner being were released and opened. He said more to her, in rare, brief moments, than he had uttered in a lifetime to others. Abigail had an extraordinary talent for making everyone feel at ease. Although it was a highly unlikely arrangement, in view of the customs and culture of their days, Abigail and Nathaniel had become friends and over the years their friendship had flourished.

While Nathaniel had no appointed times of conversation with Abigail—and certainly he *never* touched her or even came close to physical contact—still, she was his sole reason for staying on the Carmel ranch and for maintaining a nigh-impossible record of loyalty to Nabal. It was for *her* he did his best at managing and mollifying shepherds and hired hands. It was for *her* he made peace between master and servants. And it was for *her* he kept things running smoothly between others in the community and Nabal. In short, he worshiped the beautiful and very smart Abigail, and no price was too great to pay to stay within close range of her.

This morning, though, Nathaniel muttered to himself, *Nabal had gone too far!* He hurried frantically from the sheep pens to the cooking area outside the women's tents to find Abigail. By the time he found her he was sweating nervously, like a condemned man, and his breathing was uneven and painful.

As she saw Nathaniel coming, Abigail hurled a stream of instructions to one of her maids and moved out to meet him.

"What is it?" The dark purple rings under his eyes and the reddening about his sweat-drenched neck frightened her. Nathaniel was a brave man . . . accustomed to conflicts . . . and nothing, not even Nabal, disturbed his stoic poise. She understood instantly that it was no trifling matter that brought him puffing and hurrying toward her.

"Take a good look at the mountains of Judah," he panted. "This is the last day of our lives!" His voice was cryptic and hoarse.

"Why?" Abigail stared at him, knowing he was a man not given to exaggeration.

"Why?" Nathaniel shouted. "Because he has finally done it. That's why. He has doomed us all!"

Looking at the tough, grizzled, bearded man in front of her, Abigail took in a deep breath, straightened herself and said slowly and distinctly, "Nathaniel, tell me *exactly* what Nabal has done, and don't spare me the details."

The tanned, sinewy foreman turned, picked up a small stone, and flung it toward the foothills. The words from this tight-lipped man started to flow in an orderly fashion as if he were reading a litany from a scroll.

"It's been well over a year now that David and his men have protected our shepherds, the hired men, and our flocks from plunder and harm. Not so much as one lamb has been stolen because of the generous and diligent services these armed men have given Master Nabal. David's soldiers have been like brothers and family to us. Now, early this morning, David sent a traditional, time-honored request to Nabal." Nathaniel shook his head.

"Ah," Abigail exclaimed. "David wants to join our festival as a reward for his men. Right?" She asked this, her eyes sparkling with the idea of being face to face with Israel's king-elect.

"No. Nothing that grand." The man scratched at his beard absent-mindedly. "David merely asked for his 'protection fee.' He sent ten men to request a small donation out of the bounty of our shearing festival. He just wants to give his soldiers some needed rest and change of diet. After all, many of his men have not been home or seen loved ones in three years."

"So," Abigail interrupted, "my husband said no." No anger showed, but Nathaniel caught a deepening in her voice and knew that although she was disturbed, she would outwardly display no disloyalty toward Nabal.

Inwardly Abigail was far removed from her usual calm response and presence of mind, for to herself she thought irritably, *Nabal, you are such an ass.*

Nathaniel waited a moment, and then drawing closer, whispered fiercely, "It's worse. The master not only refused the men, he insulted David by bellowing, 'Who is this fellow, David? Who does this son of Jesse think he is?' "

Abigail covered her mouth with her hands. She was losing her forebearing spirit in rapid fashion.

"Then," Nathaniel went on, "Nabal ranted and rambled about runaway servants and disappearing hired hands and how they have cheated him. And why should he take bread, water, and freshly slaughtered meat away from his own hired hands to give it to a bunch of renegade nobodies who suddenly appear out of nowhere?

"Oh, I tell you, Mistress Abigail, I can see David's face when he's told all this. And I *know* it will only be a matter of hours before he marches over one of those hills and kills us all!"

Nathaniel squatted down on his haunches and said sadly, "Like I told you before, Mistress Abigail, David's men have been so good to us. We've never suffered any harm from them, not once. It's just been *good* we've received the whole time we've grazed our flocks in these hills. Those men and boys have been like a wall of protection around us, and the master's prosperity this year comes directly from the difference David and his men have made!"

Now he stood up, and taking a step or two toward Abigail, he did something he'd never done before. He took her pale and beautiful hands in his sunburned, calloused ones, and pleaded, "My friend, this is all beyond me. Please think fast. Otherwise there will be much trouble and much bloodshed. I know it. Not only for Nabal, but for you and all of us. We know he is a stubborn, ill-tempered man. No one can talk to him, but maybe you can. Will you try?"

It was almost in that same instant that she knew what she would do. "Nathaniel, I'll not talk to my husband about this matter. You have said yourself no one can talk to him. Besides, this is not the time for talk. It's time for action.

"Nabal is a fool, I grant you know that better than anyone, but he also suffers from a memory loss. He forgets that the one who asked for food today is yesterday's slayer of Goliath. And he also does not recall that David has slaughtered his 'ten thousands' of Philistines and Amalekites and to slay us would be nothing to him!

"Now, I want you to go back to your work, as if everything were just fine. Let's *both* trust Jehovah on this one. I know what I must do, and I'll get on with it. . . ."

The man's eyes were still filled with disbelief, so she added, "My friend, you'll see. It will be all right." And with that she gave him a gentle shove down the slope toward the sheep pens.

Even *before* she married Nabal, Abigail knew he was a difficult and churlish fool, but lurking in the back of her erudite and lucid mind was the idea—and the confidence— that she could handle any man, woman, or child under any circumstances. For the most part Abigail had done just that. She had developed skills as the mistress of a large and prosperous household, and her tactful wisdom was almost at lengendary proportions. Now this new challenge, perhaps the greatest of her years, loomed before her, and Abigail rose to meet it as if she'd been born for this moment.

The thought that David and several hundred of his men might be well on their way to massacre Nabal and everyone in his household sent a solitary shiver running down her spine. But she had no time for histrionics—or the opposite, quiet denial. So she resolutely said to herself, *Well, I'll do what I must. It amounts to two things. I must convince David that we are not worth the killing, and then I must feed him and his men. Oh, Jehovah, do remember I'm known as a 'woman of good understanding.' Make me clever, and lend me the armor of Your courage!*

Then, with firm, long strides, she went directly to the cooking tents. "Leah, you are in charge of tonight's meal. Cover my absence as best you can and see that all goes well." Leah, the oldest and most dependable servant Abigail had, nodded her head in silent acceptance.

"Mara, Kenturah, Judith, Cozbi," Abigail pointed at four of her best workers. "You come with me now."

Huddling with the young women like an army general with his staff, Abigail explained the problem and proposed her solutions. Together they would prepare the immense provisions of food, enough to feed a small army—David's army. The young faces lit up with excitement, and they caught the spirit of the challenge. Their eyes widened in surprise, however, as their mistress began giving them the specific dimensions of their tasks. "I think it will take a couple hundred loaves of bread, and at least two barrels of wine. The two of you get that ready." She touched the shoulder of Mara and looked at Kenturah. Obediently they nodded.

"I will take care of the meat," she said under her breath. "Five dressed, roasted lambs, maybe six."

"Mistress Abigail . . ." It was the eager-to-be-on-with-it Judith. "Roasted grain—will one bushel be enough?"

"No. It's better to take more and leave it with David's men than to run out. Two bushels."

Abigail then took the tiny hands of her shyest servant girl, Cozbi. Trying to draw her out, she asked, "It wouldn't do to send a feast like this without something for their sweet tooth, now, would it?"

The girl smiled and said softly, "It's raisin clusters and honeyed fig cakes, right?" Abigail gave her a quick hug and answered, "Yes. About a hundred clusters and at least two hundred cakes."

Because she was used to running a large household, she had as much food as possible prepared well in advance of this shearing time, and she had the utmost confidence in these young servant maids of hers, Abigail knew it would be only a matter of hours before the food would be assembled. She headed off in the direction of the fragrant baking pits where servants were turning and basting young lambs on spits over the hot coals.

When Nathaniel was told that Abigail needed four of his men to accompany a donkey train of food to David's men, he slapped his thigh, uttered, "Ah ha!" and permitted a slight smile to cross his lips. *I don't know the whole plan, but what I do know, I like!* he said to himself. And for the first time since early morning, his breathing evened out in a somewhat normal pattern.

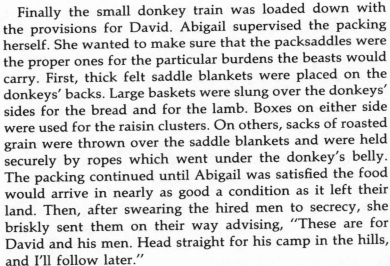

Finally the small donkey train was loaded down with the provisions for David. Abigail supervised the packing herself. She wanted to make sure that the packsaddles were the proper ones for the particular burdens the beasts would carry. First, thick felt saddle blankets were placed on the donkeys' backs. Large baskets were slung over the donkeys' sides for the bread and for the lamb. Boxes on either side were used for the raisin clusters. On others, sacks of roasted grain were thrown over the saddle blankets and were held securely by ropes which went under the donkey's belly. The packing continued until Abigail was satisfied the food would arrive in nearly as good a condition as it left their land. Then, after swearing the hired men to secrecy, she briskly sent them on their way advising, "These are for David and his men. Head straight for his camp in the hills, and I'll follow later."

"Mistress, may we go with you?" Mara and Kenturah volunteered. Abigail's smile reflected her gratitude for their loyalty in this time of uncertainty. They all understood that the trip could be dangerous because of David's wrath toward Nabal, and yet, even so, the two servant girls wanted to be with her.

"Thank you for asking, but no. You stay here." She explained, "I think the master might suspect something if too many people are missing from tonight's feast." Actually she was hoping Nabal would be too preoccupied with his drinking to notice anybody's absence. And besides, the frenzied preparations of the morning and the loading of that much food had consumed all her energies. She needed to be alone to organize her thoughts. The ride would give her time to do exactly that.

Abigail waited until the men and donkeys were near the lower foothills, and then she mounted what Nathaniel promised to be a gentle animal.

Alone, and thoroughly enjoying it, she rode out into the rugged mountain country. The beauty of the valley behind her and the rocks and trees beyond and above made time pass quickly. Every once in awhile she heard the high cry of a bird's call or caught the distant tinkling of the bells of the donkey caravan.

But as Abigail reflected on the task before her, she was tempted to dismount this patient beast and do what Nabal did—escape into the wineskins and deny the reality of life's crises. *How wonderful it would be to stay here, to let the cool mountain breezes blow through my hair, and to never go any farther up the mountain nor turn and go back down to the valley*, she thought.

After a few moments, though, Abigail, whose mind was as astute as her face was beautiful, shook her head, as if to clear it, and began reckoning with the immediate concerns of her mission. Actually she had three major concerns—Nabal, King Saul, and David.

Nabal was the most obvious. She'd known, after years of being his wife, that there were times when silence before acting on a decision of her own was absolutely best. But, because she was still Nabal's wife, he would have to be told. *But that could come later,* she thought. *Much later.*

"Now, King Saul scares me," she said aloud to the twitching ears of her donkey. "He's unpredictable about most things and people. But not about people who *help* David! Did you know, my four-footed friend, that the king ordered the wholesale massacre of Ahimelech and eighty-five other priests and all their families because they had helped David?" The donkey hesitated before going around a small boulder, and Abigail, with a quick laugh, said, "I see. You want to go back, too." She rode along in silence for a few moments wondering what kind of devastation King Saul would bring down about her if word ever reached him about today's attempt to aid the outlaw-fugitive David.

Finally she said respectfully, "As to Israel's hero, well, I've committed us to this, and I will meet with the undaunted David." Abigail patted the donkey's neck more to encourage herself than the beast and resumed, "But listen, you never come suddenly or abruptly face to face with a man who is angry. A man like that must not be surprised, lest he use his sword first and seek the truth later. That, my friend, is why I have sent the caravan ahead of us."

The winding trail reached the summit on the main foothill and widened out onto a small plain. It was there she caught her first glimpse of the men who fought side by side with the legendary king-elect. Marching toward her were hundreds of men, and even at a distance she could tell they were dressed for battle—sword or dagger strapped to their side or chest. It was a sight that chilled her to the bone. But remembering her mission, she realized that somewhere in that mass of men was David himself—David, the man all of the women of Israel praised and adored; David, the brave man Israeli men respected and followed.

Abigail urged her donkey forward, her eyes searching the ranks of the approaching army for signs of their leader. It wouldn't be long now before she would be talking with David ben Jesse.

When David's ten scouts had come back with Nabal's obnoxious refusal, the warrior instantly strapped on his own sword and bellowed, "Get your swords!" Six hundred men obeyed. "Keep two hundred men here to guard our gear," he ordered, and then without further word, David and four hundred angry men marched out of camp to murder Nabal and all his people.

So intent on their vengeful mission, David and his troops paid no attention to the passing donkey train obviously laden with food. David's thoughts raged: *A lot of good it did us to help this fellow. We protected his flocks, up here in the mountains and in the wilderness, so that not one animal was lost or stolen, but he has repaid me bad for good. All that I get for my trouble is insults. May God curse me if even one of his men remains alive by tomorrow morning!*

But then, way out in the distance David saw the woman. With interest he watched her even as her eyes searched for him among the front lines, and as the distance between them narrowed, her beauty all but overwhelmed him.

He had always praised Jehovah for making women so vastly different from men, and this was especially true during the last three years, as he spent the bulk of his time with six hundred men. At any rate, he considered himself a fair and accurate judge of womanly beauty, and even at a distance he could tell that this woman was exceptionally beautiful.

David assessed her fine flaxen clothing, the colorful embroidery embellishment at the neck and sleeves, and the sparkle of gold about her ears and wrists and decided that either she was the spoiled daughter of a wealthy rancher or the pampered wife of a nobleman. *But what is she doing way out here?* he wondered.

Her eyes finally singled him out, and almost unconsciously David nodded his head to affirm his identity. But her next move astounded him. Before he could say anything, this beautiful woman slid off the donkey and there, in all her finery, flattened herself on the grassy ground before his feet. *The woman has beauty and wealth. But humility also?* he questioned to himself.

David touched her shoulder and told her to rise, but she would only kneel. So there before him was a picture of pure beauty and refined courtesy. David was completely captivated. *Who is she?* he wondered.

As if she read his mind, she said with a calm, clear voice, "My name is Abigail. Wife of Nabal." She waited a moment for the names to make an impact on the warrior, and then she continued, "I willingly accept all the blame in this matter, my lord. Your anger with my husband is justified. But before you take another step, please stay a moment and listen to what I have to say."

Her face, so appealing, and her hands folded in supplication with her fingers just touching the tips of her chin, had already taken the urgency out of David's desire for vengeance. "Go on," he commanded quietly.

"David, my lord, my husband Nabal is everything you think he is—churlish and foul-tempered. But don't pay any attention to what he said. He is a fool, just as his name implies. And I, your handmaiden, did not see the young men you sent. I was not told of your message until later this morning. So, my lord, as the Lord Almighty lives, and as your soul lives—seeing that the Lord has kept you from murdering and taking vengeance into your own hands—I pray by the life of God, that all your enemies shall be as cursed as Nabal is." There was no mistaking the sincerity and purpose of Abigail's motives as she waited at David's feet.

Then she continued, "I beg you to accept my gift of food for you and the young men who follow you."

"The donkey train we passed. Was that from you?" David asked.

"Yes, my lord." Her face brightened.

"This was all your idea?"

She nodded and said softly, "I did not even tell my husband. Forgive me for my boldness in sending the food and in coming out here, but I had to." Now she rose before him and was only an arm's length away when she said distinctly so that he *and* his men could hear, "Jehovah will surely reward you with eternal royalty for your descendants, for you are fighting His battles, and evil has not been found in you in all your life. Even when you are chased by those who seek your life, you are safe in the care of the Lord your God, just as though you were safe inside His shepherd's scrip." Abigail pointed to David's belt and the goatskin pouch which he always tied there. It pleased her that he held the time-honored tradition of carrying such a humble reminder of his shepherding days. Then, remembering the stories of Goliath's death at the hands of David, she continued, "The lives of your enemies shall disappear like stones from a sling!"

David was now beginning to marvel at the workings of her mind. She was talking to him on his level and her logic was astounding, but he was completely beguiled by her next words. "My lord David, when Jehovah has done all the good things He promised you and has made you king of Israel, you won't want the conscience of a murderer who took the law into his own hands."

She paused, and David realized she had touched on what was most dear to his heart. Her words had penetrated to the core of his honor and had awakened it with new life.

"And when the Lord has done these great things for you," she was saying softly, "please remember me."

The noise of David's slap against his sword belt and the sudden outburst of his laughter startled Abigail, but the next words he spoke warmed every part of her. "Bless the Lord God of Israel who has sent you to meet me today!" he shouted. "Bless you for keeping me from murdering the man and carrying out vengeance with my own hands." Then lowering his voice a little he advised, "For I swear by Jehovah, the God of Israel who has kept me from hurting you, that if you had not come out to meet me, not one of Nabal's men would have been alive tomorrow morning."

Turning for a second, he motioned two of his men to come forward. To one he gave the command to return the men to camp, and the other David ordered to see to the woman's safety on the return trip home.

Then David took Abigail's hands in his, lifted them, and kissed them saying, "My lady Abigail, I accept your hospitable gifts for myself and my men. Now, return home without fear. I will not come near your husband."

They stood there facing each other. It was only an instant longer, but in that moment Abigail felt her heart give way with a torrent of love for this man. This man, once a shepherd boy but now a hunted fugitive would no doubt someday be king of Israel. Quickly though, she shoved those thoughts and feelings down inside her and remounted her donkey.

As Abigail and her soldier-escort moved in the direction of Carmel, a murky gray darkness pushed in and obscured the last deep pink colors of twilight behind the mountains. Night was falling, and a sudden rush of wind not far above her head told Abigail that a sparrow hawk or a falcon was winging his way to his roosting place in the rocks. But it wasn't long before they were near the edges of Nabal's land. Here Abigail bid her accompanying soldier farewell, and the donkey, pleased to be on familiar ground, broke into an ambling trot along the path that led to the tents of home.

Abigail could hear the noisy exuberance of hungry men eating, drinking, and singing songs long before she saw their campfires. She was circling around the back edges of the tents to slip in unnoticed when Nathaniel stepped out of the shadows and pulled in the donkey's reins.

"Mistress Abigail, are you all right?" He peered at her in the darkness, his raspy voice full of concern.

"Yes, I'm fine. But please, help me get down." She took his hand and slid stiffly out of the saddle. Wearily she whispered, "It's been a long, long day, my friend! And now I fear comes the worst part."

"No, you don't have to face him tonight." Even in the dim light she could see a look of triumph in Nathaniel's face.

"But Nabal needs to know what I've done."

"In the morning perhaps. But not now."

"Nathaniel, you rascal," she teased, "what have you done?"

"Why, nothing Mistress. Only the master decided to have

an extra big celebration tonight. I saw to it that he had no lack of wineskins."

Abigail smiled and shook her head. "I'm grateful, Nathaniel." She patted his shoulders by way of a polite dismissal, but still he stood before her, his hands anxiously twisting the donkey's tethering straps.

"Oh, forgive me," she blurted out. "You want to know how it went with David? Well, let's see . . ." she began, trying to quickly condense everything because her strength was so spent. "I just told David he didn't want my husband's blood on his hands or on his conscience when he becomes king. That's all."

Nathaniel whistled through his teeth and said in awe, "Mistress, you are a wonder. A beautiful wonder!"

"No, I'm a *tired* wonder. Where is Cozbi or Mara?"

"Here, Mistress Abigail," they said in unison.

Gratefully she surrendered herself to the nurturing hands of her two maids.

The sheep from one of Nabal's largest flocks were being dunked and given their cleansing baths as quickly as possible in large water troughs before being sheared. The process was advancing as fast as could be expected. Men and animals alike were wet, and tiny lambs bleated shrilly and piteously for their mothers. It all added up to a confusing,

chaotic morning. The hired hands and shepherds eased
the severity of their back-breaking work by hurling hu-
morously crude insults at each other. And the loud racket
of men and sheep at times was almost deafening.

Abigail shielded her eyes from the brightness of the midmorning sun and, after finding Nabal, she shouted above
the din, "My lord, I need to speak to you."

The men's bantering ceased. And except for the common-
place sounds of several hundred sheep and the wind rustling
through the feathery branches of the tamarisk trees, everything quieted.

Nabal, his back still toward her, whined in his usual irk-
some way, "Now what does the woman want?" He flung
his arms upward in a gesture of mock helplessness. "Haven't
I given her everything she desires? Doesn't she live and
dress in a luxury few women ever know? Haven't I given
her an abundance of servant girls? Yet she still *wants* something!" He finally turned and stared at her with beady,
black eyes full of contempt.

Preferring to ignore his unrelenting rudeness and wanting
to preserve what little dignity he still possessed in front
of his men, she asked respectfully, "My husband, may we
go over there and talk privately?" Abigail pointed to a small
grove of fig trees a few yards up the slope. Within herself
she reasoned that the grove, which she had cultivated and
nurtured to bear fruit each August, might also grant them
a measure of privacy and a gentle setting for the May morning.

"What?" Nabal groaned like the camels do when they
have to get on their feet. "Nathaniel, didn't you tell this
woman that it's sheep-shearing season? I've better things
to do than take a leisurely stroll with her." Then directly
to Abigail he muttered with much rancor, "You have something to say, woman, you say it right here . . . now. And
be quick about it!" At this moment Nabal was struck by
the fact that his men were listening and standing idle. He
vented a stream of curses at them, and then in a voice

that rebounded against the nearest hillside he roared, "You lazy dogs, get to your tasks. This is none of your business!"

He wiped the sweat off his face with his sleeve, dried his hands on the folds of the cloth girdle about his waist, and walked over to his wife.

"Speak," he demanded.

Nabal stood before her, feet planted firmly apart and arms folded defensively over his chest. His breath, rotten and soured from all-night drinking, assaulted Abigail's senses. But she turned her head slightly, drew a deep breath and said, "As you wish, my lord."

She knew the time had come to confront her husband with just exactly how close his insulting refusal of David's request had come to jeopardizing all of their lives. It was also time to confess her secret part in all this. Just beyond Nabal's shoulder she caught the eye of Nathaniel and, feeling a surge of support from this old friend, she summoned up new courage.

I must remember that strong, bitter truths have to be sweetened with the honey of gentleness or they will not be swallowed, she thought. And so, with no maliciousness or spirit of resentment or criticism, the woman known for her beauty and good understanding, began to relate the events of yesterday's encounter with David. She spoke with calm, indisputable honesty, a gentle meekness of spirit, and a frightfully pounding heart.

Abigail had finished the part of the story about the message of David's ten men and Nabal's refusal and was almost to the part describing her meeting with David on the mountain trail when something began happening to Nabal.

He was no longer standing defiantly before her. Now his arms hung limply at his sides and he stooped forward in an awkward stance. His face began to lose the crimson-colored rage that had flared earlier when his wife told about the provisions and the donkey caravan. Nabal's mouth went slack and vile smelling drool ran down into his heavy black beard. His glassy, blood-veined eyes protruded beneath his bushy eyebrows in a frightening way, and as they all watched, an ashen gray pallor spread malignantly over his face. It was a terrifying sight.

Nabal fell in a crumpled mound before Abigail could catch him or even cry out for help.

In the short interval of time it took Nathaniel and two shepherds to get the master from the field to his tent, everyone who crowded around was shocked by the sudden onset of his illness.

This was a man no one would miss or mourn. But no one would forget the folly of Nabal's life, for hired hands, shepherds, maidservants, and Abigail as well, were instantly aware of the terribly swift hand of God's vengeance. The lesson they learned that day in those brief moments greatly increased their fear and awe of Jehovah.

"Is he dead yet?" someone whispered from the back edges of the tent.

"No, he lives . . . but barely," a man's voice answered.

Abigail, her beautiful brown eyes tearless but wide with wonder, anxiously pondered what was happening. She knelt beside him. He was alive, but it was as though somehow, Nabal's heart or inner core of him had died. Even as the men laid him down on his bedding, Nabal's body was beginning to stiffen. She touched him now and quickly drew away her hand. He was alive all right, but his skin was cold and he had become as solid as a petrified stone.

"Tell everyone to leave, Nathaniel. I'll stay with him." Abigail's voice was tinged with a somber dignity and a new, deliberate authority.

Slowly the tent was cleared of people. Some servants, as they moved outside, murmured their opinion that the mistress should let the old fool die alone. It would serve him right. Others, who knew Abigail better, marveled that she would continue her loyalty to Nabal, as always, even though now he was powerless to demand it.

The truth was that even as they had been carrying Nabal to his tent, Abigail had decided she would stand by him.

Nothing much has changed here, she thought. *Nabal is going to be as rigid in his dying as he was in his living.*

"So my final vigil has begun," she commented softly to Nabal, whose only response was the labored wheezings of his breathing.

"It's strange, my lord, but in our marriage you never allowed me to speak my mind. Now you have no choice. There's no place to run and hide from me, no wineskins to escape into. There are just the two of us here, and only I can speak." There was no vindictiveness or condemnation in her whispered words, only a lavender sadness which colored her voice at the thoughts of what their marriage might have been.

Years before, Abigail had accepted her husband's coarse, repugnant, and foolish nature as being uniquely his—much like other men possessed virtuous and honorable traits. Nabal, she reasoned, was very different from most people she knew. To her thinking, he was a person of limited and distorted vision. When he saw sordid, debased behavior in others, he lowered himself to their vile depths. What placed him, as a youth, on these self-destructive paths she never knew—only that at the time of their marriage what flames of decency still flickered and burned in Nabal's conscience and heart were soon put out and quickly quenched by the ever-increasing amounts of wine he consumed.

"My husband," she said softly and without malice, "do you know of the proverb which says a man betrays himself as a fool in three ways? He shows his true fool's character when his money is touched, when he is in a rage, and when he is in his cups." She put her hand on Nabal's forehead.

"Unfortunately, yesterday you betrayed yourself as a fool in all three areas. Oh, Nabal, don't you wish you could go back and relive your yesterdays?" Abigail smiled ruefully. "No, I don't suppose you do," she said as she answered her own question.

In the days and nights that followed, Abigail left Nabal's side only when she had to. Leah brought her meals on a tray and scolded her mistress when food was left virtually untouched.

Abigail did what she could for her desperately ill husband, changing the cooling wet cloths on his brow and trying to coax little swallows of barley broth between his parched lips, but it was all to no avail. For ten days and nights he hung suspended somewhere between life and death.

Then as the sun set on the eleventh day, Abigail was startled by a new sound from him. Thinking he was trying to speak to her, she put her head on Nabal's chest. But he said nothing. The sound was only the soft gurgling voice of death.

In a few moments, Nabal the fool was no more.

Nathaniel himself went to David's camp with the message of Nabal's death.

"My lord," he bowed low before David, "I have come with important news from my mistress, Abigail."

"Let's hear it," David said as he continued to sharpen the edges of his sword.

"My master, Nabal, is dead and buried, and my mistress sends you this message, 'Vengeance is always best when left in Jehovah's hands. See, the Lord that lives has killed Nabal so you and your throne are not soiled by his blood. Praise the God of our fathers!' "

David jumped up, raised his sword high above his head and shouted out in a whoop of joy, "Did you hear that, men? God has killed the fool. Praise God! He has kept me from the killing, and now Nabal has received punishment for his sins."

Then to Nathaniel he declared, "Your mistress understood this whole matter. What a woman of wisdom and beauty she is!"

"There is something else, my lord," Nathaniel ventured.

"More from Abigail?"

"No, my lord . . ."

"Then what?"

"It is just that I am old, but my times with Nabal and these rugged mountains have toughened me, and I'm strong in many ways. . . ." Nathaniel paused.

"And?"

"I desire to fight with you and your men, my lord. And I swear, by Jehovah's name, that I will be a loyal, faithful soldier to the future king of Israel." Nathaniel fairly glowed with his newly found military fervor.

David stepped back and surveyed the sinewy bear of a man and said, "I see. Then tell me, old man, can you act on an order right now?"

"Yes sir! my lord."

David nodded. "Fine. Then go back to your mistress, Abigail."

The man looked as if a donkey had kicked the wind squarely out of him.

"Go, go . . . go back?" he stammered.

"Yes," David said calmly. "That's my command, and when you get there give your mistress, Abigail, this message. Tell her I wish to marry her, and ask her if she will become my wife. When she says yes, put the best man in charge of managing all of Abigail's lands and flocks and help her to assemble her things. Then, pack your personal gear, accompany your mistress here, and join me and my men."

Nathaniel was shocked by David's ability to make such

decisions—and so quickly. His master, Nabal, had been quite the opposite.

"Sir?" The old man's face was still wreathed in concern. "Yes?"

"What if she says no?"

Things were moving too swiftly for Nathaniel, so he completely missed the small, mischievous smile which played for just an instant across David's handsome face.

Israel's king-elect leaned close to Nathaniel's sunburned face and ended the discussion by whispering, "What makes you think she'll say no?"

"Oh, yes, sir! Very true, my lord!" he shouted, as it dawned on him that there wasn't a woman in all of Israel who would say no to this man. And the idea of Abigail and David together and married brought him so much joy that he knew if he'd been one of Nabal's sheep dogs, he would have wagged his tail.

Nathaniel never remembered much from his fast, bone-bruising donkey ride down from David's camp. And he was not surprised that Abigail accepted David's proposal, but he never forgot the incredible speed with which his mistress settled her affairs.

In fact, it was just a little humiliating that by the time he'd given orders to various men about continuing the work of the ranch and was going back to help her, Abigail had no need of his services.

There she was, along with her maids—Leah, Mara, Kentura, Judith, and Cozbi—all packed, saddled on donkeys, and ready to go. And she wasn't even out of breath.

Nathaniel burned with devotion for this woman of great beauty and wisdom. *She will make a wonderful wife for David. May they have many children,* he thought. And slapping the donkey's rump, they set off for David's camp.

Following and serving David, the dashing fugitive-hero of their times, left a great deal to be desired when Nathaniel really got into the doing of it. He'd fancied himself fighting gallantly for the glory of Israel when, in reality, his army service found him participating in one raiding party after another; killing every person in sight, and stealing everything from the enemy but the stones of their cooking fires.

Nathaniel had also enjoyed envisioning his mistress Abigail and David living peaceably without Nabal's harrassment in the picturesque mountains around Carmel. Instead, for the first year of their marriage, they were billeted first in the city of Gath, and then in Ziklag, in the heart of Philistine country.

But of all Nathaniel's hopes for Abigail, the one that suffered the most was the dream of his mistress being David's *only* wife. He was shocked to learn, soon after he'd joined the band of men, that Ahino-am, a woman from Jezreel, was *already* married to David.

Slowly the pedestal that held David in Nathaniel's mind began to crumble. It was best, in the long run, that the tough old man never knew the full extent of the souring of his honey-sweet visions. Nor did he live long enough to learn of the dire anguish Abigail would be forced to endure.

For at the exact time Nathaniel was off raiding a Geshurite town with David and his men, the Amalekites decided to avenge their dead. They raided David's home camp in Ziklag, plundered its possessions, burned the city to the ground, and with bloodthirsty cries of victory, carried off all the women and children—including Nathaniel's beloved mistress, Abigail.

Killing the inhabitants of the Geshurite town was Nathaniel's last encounter with David, his men, wars, and battlefields for it was on the edges of that town that he was gravely wounded. And while he lay dying that long, cold night after the battle, he spent the time reviewing the chronicles of his life.

Euphorically, and sometimes without substantial reality, Nathaniel recalled the memories of Carmel as he wanted to remember them. The foul stench of the burning and the dying made him yearn for the familiar odors of men and animals at Nabal's sheep pens. The lifetime of ranching always meant the sweat of men mixed with the aroma of garlic and the earthy smell of sheep dung. He longed for one more day in those sheep pens, but knowing it would never be possible, he pushed his mind to remember other things.

Deliberately, he reconstructed some of the open-hearted conversations he'd had with Abigail while he was Nabal's overseer. As he pictured her beautiful face, his throat tightened with unabashed admiration. And with amazing lucidness, he recalled the day his lovely Abigail had used her head and saved all their lives. It was truly remarkable the way she had ministered to the needs of David and his men. Nathaniel managed a wan smile when he recalled that there was no period of mourning for Nabal after his death. Once he had delivered David's offer of marriage, Abigail had been *instantly* ready to leave Carmel and join David.

Nathaniel's last memories, in the darkness of that night, began to blur in his mind. He tried to tell the soldier lying next to him about his own naively innocent ideas regarding soldiering and wars—how enthusiasm had bubbled over in him the day he volunteered for David's army. But the soldier was already a corpse.

Finally, as he grew weaker, he sentimentally rambled on about Abigail's marriage to David. Then in his last hour, as the blood drained from his wounded groin and his life ebbed, Nathaniel consoled and warmed himself by believing that soon all would be well.

This day will be another victory for David. Abigail is waiting for us in Ziklag, and David will soon be the rightful king. He'll make Abigail the queen . . . his only queen, and we'll all live happily. And so his mind conjured up rose-colored hope until the last breath of life passed between his lips.

Nathaniel never knew that, in reality, David had other ways, and Jehovah had other plans.

David and four hundred of his men finally caught up

with the Amalekites who had devastated their city and stolen their wives and children. Then for two nights and one
long, bloody day, they ruthlessly, and without deliberation,
slaughtered the Amalekites; no one escaped their wrath except several hundred of the enemy troops who fled on
camels. David and his men rescued the Israeli women and
children, including his wives Ahino-am and Abigail, but
many of the women had been brutalized and raped.

"My Abigail . . . Abigail. What have they done?" David
moaned as he beheld Abigail after she was finally found
and rescued. Streaks of white appeared through her dark,
disheveled hair. Deep, blackened circles underlined her eyes,
and a haunted look, which was to stay for months, implied
that the darkest of memories were haunting her soul.

Whether Abigail had been attacked and raped by the
Amalekites, no one ever knew for sure, for she never spoke
of those tragic days. But there's no doubt her outstanding
beauty would have set her apart as a most rare prize in
the hands of the enemy.

After David recovered everything that had been taken
from him by the Amalekites—because horrors seem to wait
together in bunches until they have strength in numbers,
and *then* they invade our lives—he was dealt yet another
blow. For just as David was dealing with his losses on the
homefront, King Saul, all his sons (including David's dearest
friend, Jonathan), and scores of Israelis were killed in a
battle with the Philistines on Mount Gilboa.

Events raced frantically forward, and within a few days
David was crowned king of all Israel. He established himself
and his kingdom in the city of Hebron. And it was there,
a couple of years later, that Abigail gave birth to her only
child, a son named Chileab, David's second son.

The events of David and Abigail's lives were not quite
so practically and romantically lived out as Nathaniel had
envisioned. However, he would have been pleased to have
known that, in the last fifteen years of Abigail's life, a deep
settled joy returned to her beautiful, but aged countenance.

For, though still married to David and the mother of his child, she came to a peaceful and purposeful acceptance of her life and her decisions. With David's loving permission, she chose to spend her remaining years, not in Hebron or Jerusalem, but on the Carmel land she'd always loved.

Nathaniel would have rested more comfortably in his grave had he known that the ending of Abigail's life was infinitely more wonderful than the beginning or the middle, as it ofttimes is with Jehovah's plans.

PART V

Bathsheba

"Then David comforted Bath-sheba;
and when he slept with her, she
conceived and gave birth to a
son and named him Solomon."

2 Samuel 12:24

*W*ill the wars begin again, now that it is spring?" both the young officers questioned their commander.

Uriah, finishing off the last of the wine from his goblet, shook his head and answered, "Yes, and we will probably get our orders within the next two weeks." He paused and looked out over the rooftops of Jerusalem. Then almost to himself he added, "That foolish quarrel with King Hanun's officers started the war last year, and I just have a feeling in my bones that King David is out to finish the Ammonites for good this time. The army of Israel will march soon . . . mark my words." The large man stood up, stretched his long legs, and surveyed the city as night dropped its curtains around them.

Uriah had relished the excellent home-cooked delicacies served earlier; it was a most welcome change from the utilitarian sameness of army food. And the camaraderie of his two junior officers plus the presence of his beautiful wife had put him in a satisfied and mellowed mood. They had eaten downstairs and now they were enjoying the coolness of Uriah's rooftop. Their conversation time was spent on catching up on Jerusalem trivia, local gossip, rumors, and other bits of information that escaped them while off on their military assignments. Uriah and his men were among the elite Jerusalem militia that had been sent the year before to train and lead the twenty thousand Syrian mercenaries King David had hired from the lands of Rehob and Zobah to help fight the Ammonite war. Time at home had been very rare, and tonight the men suspected their "Jerusalem time" was running out once more.

Now, with the light, cooling winds prevailing and the black velvet covering of the starlit sky, the men had finally come to the subject of the *next* war. All of them had known they would.

In fact, the word *war* had been burning in their minds like a silent glowing coal of fire, and even Bathsheba wondered just how long it would be before they had enough of inconsequential chatter and would talk of what filled their souls—army life and battles.

She understood exactly what it meant to be a military wife. *I didn't marry one man,* she smiled to herself and thought, *I married the whole army.* Being married to the army meant learning the rules and accepting, like a soldier, the responsibilities and the setbacks. But, most of all, it meant adjusting to loving and living with a man in absentia. Uriah seemed to thrive on his wartime excursions. He and his men were born soldiers. They lived to be warriors. Bathsheba admired the way they understood the art of the battles they fought, how they believed in the justice of the wars they won, and she knew about the stern joy which warriors feel when their enemies lie defeated in great numbers before them. But mostly she marveled at the fact that her husband and his men needed nothing more in their lives than a rousing cause to fight for and defend on some distant battlefield and an unshakable, reliable woman to keep the home fires burning. *Why aren't my needs that simple?* she often questioned within herself.

Jerusalem was not a large city but one set on the brink of rugged hills and encircled by lush green palm groves and vine-covered valleys and ravines. It was not Uriah's hometown, for he was born a Hittite, a foreign mercenary who volunteered his services. But he had come up through the ranks of David's army, pledged his alliance to the king, and loved the bustling magnificence of Jerusalem more than any other city he had ever seen. "I will always, till the day I die, fight to save this place and perpetuate the glory of David's kingdom," he had often stated with fierce pride. And always, just before leaving for any tour of duty, Uriah parted with his wife by saying, "My king needs me, but I'll return to you, my love." As his words lingered in her mind she wondered, *Well, King David needs you, but what about me? Uriah, will you ever need me?* But she did not deem it appropriate to speak these thoughts aloud to Uriah.

Now, climbing the stairs with a fresh jug of wine, Bathsheba heard them talking of war, and a sudden wave of discontent swept over her. *So it is another war,* she thought as she refilled their goblets. How she wished Uriah and his men wouldn't talk so eagerly of going off to war! And as on other occasions, she was tempted to ask Uriah, "Am I such a bad wife that you prefer the company of your men to mine?" But in that instant her eyes met Uriah's and though they danced with excitement over the prospect of war, she could also see that the excitement was for her, too. She smiled wistfully to herself, remembering the scratch of his beard as he nuzzled her neck in their more private moments.

She touched his shoulder in a gesture of love and thought, *No, you don't prefer the army's company to mine. But you are a brave, self-restrained, loyal soldier, and a part of you will always be restless and eager to serve the king.* Often Uriah had whispered, even as he held her in his arms, how when he was "out there" fighting in the field, he had dreamed of being at home with her. Yet when he *was* home, she knew all too well that a part of him was still "out there" with his men, somewhere on the battlefield. Part of the proof of her logic lay in the fact that, while they had been married for several years, she still did not possess the two things she wanted above all else: to be needed by him and to have children.

Easily she had evaded her Jerusalem neighbor's pointed questions. She hated the looks of other women who by their eyes asked what she had done to be barren and so cursed of God. But sometimes the prying, relentless interrogations from the women who were wives of men in the select inner circle of King David's court were more than difficult to side-step. It was downright impossible. Often it was none too subtly suggested that because of her astounding beauty and Uriah's handsome features, their children would be glorious examples of pulchritude, so why didn't she get on with it?

The truth for Uriah was simply that the importance of having children came after the importance of serving his king. Fondly he had promised, "There will be a time, my darling Bathsheba, when you will have our children, but for now I have pledged myself to our king." And with those words he always felt comfortable as he left their spacious Jerusalem house. "Our very empty house," Bathsheba would mutter aloud to Vesta, her maidservant, for days after he was gone.

This night she shoved her thoughts aside and listened to Uriah as he warmed to his favorite subject. He was saying, "Under David, the once feeble Hebrew nation, which any neighboring tribe could humble, has now become a first-rate power!" The officers raised their goblets in a salute to the truth. "We are respected by all the peoples around us," he continued. "Our King David has expanded Israel's borders and established extensive trade routes. In his more than thirty years as king, David has taken the broken pieces of Israel, the northern and southern tribes, and molded them together into one mighty nation." Uriah brought both his large hands together and intermeshed his fingers for emphasis. "The Hebrews," he went on, "are stronger now, militar-

ily, than they were back in Joshua's fighting days, and the
Israelis are more spiritually in tune with their God than
they have ever been under anyone else's leadership."

How a man of so few private words could be so eloquent
publicly about his king was beyond her. And because none
of what Uriah was saying was new to her, Bathsheba impa-
tiently brought everyone back to present realities with, "My
lord, Uriah, when I pray to Jehovah for your safety and
your victories, which battlefield will you be on this time?"
Her voice, deep and sensual, hung on the night air, sending
unseen shivers down the young soldiers' backs, and they
found new ways to envy their commanding officer. Uriah
did not miss their reaction, and turning to look at Bathsheba
he took her hand.

Even during the day when she was in the brilliant, all-
revealing sunlight, Bathsheba's face and form were nothing
short of flawless perfection. Her thick, brown, wavy hair,
now tinted with a reddish glow from the henna rinse he
had brought home from one of his military jaunts to Egypt,
was piled up on top of her head. Little gold and mother-
of-pearl combs held it in place, but a few wayward tendrils
framed her face in an unruly fashion which only served
to make her more lovely. Her white dress, a marvelous
contrast to her hair, was of a soft, alluring fabric trimmed
in tiny gold beads; and every once in awhile a breeze caught
a sleeve or the hem and defined the voluptuous contours
of her body. But, if she was a beauty in the revealing light
of the sun, Uriah reasoned, by the moon's light she gained
an ethereal, heavenly glow.

In those moments, this soldier—one of King David's
toughest, most iron-willed commanders—thought his heart
would burst for the tender love he felt for his beautiful
wife. And what wounded him even more severely was his
knowledge that no matter how hard he tried, he seemed
to be incapable of expressing his deepest feelings for her.
Or worse, when he did try, his efforts were more dishearten-

ing and clumsy than the tactical efforts of one of the most immature soldiers under his command. Uriah was confused and puzzled by the ways of women. What did Bathsheba want or need from him? How often he had wished for the words or the way to penetrate her soul. His very bones ached with the loving of her, but he could never say it.

Even now, when he vaguely sensed that her question went far deeper than which battlefield he'd be on, Uriah knew he should dispel her fears and confirm his overwhelming love for her, and yet he retreated to a safe subject. With much military brusqueness, he said, "Well, knowing Joab as I do, the general will probably aim to crush the Ammonites' heart first. So I think he'll strike at their capital city, Rabbah." He waited for a moment and then caught Bathsheba's look of resignation. *Good for you,* he thought proudly, *you take orders better than any man in the army.* Desperately he longed to come right out with it and thank her for accepting, so quickly, his army career and his call to the battlefield. But he could not. With a deep yearning, he would have loved to have composed or sung a song to her goodness, or written a poetic letter to her loveliness, but as usual he remained silent. *I'm no singer or writer,* he thought dejectedly, *I am only what I am . . . a soldier,* and he inwardly cursed his wooden tongue.

Uriah's complacent trust in his wife's ability to accept the rigors of army separations was soundly shattered later that night. He had, with great tenderness, taken her to his bed; and, while he was memorizing the fragrance of her skin and the feel of her body, she stunned his senses by whispering in the darkness, "My love, don't go to Rabbah. Please, assign someone else to go, but don't leave me here. Please, please . . ."

She had never before interfered with his work. He was, at once, both confused and touched by her request. He tightened his arms around her. "You know I can't possibly stay. I will be commanded to go. A soldier has no choice.

My king needs me . . . you know that better than most people."

Instantly, he felt her body stiffen in his arms, and in one quick movement she slipped out of his embrace. "What's wrong?" he called after her. "Where are you going?" Though he couldn't see her, she must have been standing in the doorway for he clearly heard the vexation in her voice as she said angrily in distinct, measured words, "Just once . . . just once I wish you'd ask me what *I* want."

Uriah was astounded! Bathsheba had never even hinted that she felt any resentment over his absences while on army maneuvers or battles. She had certainly never asked him to stay at home. For him to do so would be desertion. He'd be guilty of treason. *Didn't she understand that? How could she plead for such a thing? What was wrong with her?* He strained his mind for answers, but none came.

She didn't return to their bed, and sleep became impossible for Uriah. "I should go to her," he said aloud to no one. But the deeply entrenched disciplines of his army life and his devotion to King David were like chains which bound him to stay right where he was.

Even in the gray, predawn light he still could not go to her or change his plans. He longed to find her and say what he knew she wanted to hear, to watch her eyes kindle in love for him; but the chains . . . the chains were stronger, and bound him tightly to his mission. He would bivouac with his battalion of men until the king declared war. *It was best,* he reasoned, *to be on secure and familiar territory when all else was in the confusion of conflict.*

Strangely enough the logic of his thoughts did not assuage his fears or mollify and heal his hurts. And as he stepped outside into the brisk, morning breeze, he wondered if winning all the battles he'd won was worth the losing of one fine wife. In those moments it seemed to Uriah that the military achievements of his life lacked a whole lot in the comparison, but the chains of his sense of duty were locked firmly in place about him, and without a backward glance Uriah headed toward the city's gates and the army tents just beyond.

———— // ————

Because of the unusually heavy rains of the previous winter, spring burst upon Jerusalem and its surrounding hillsides with an intensity of greening and flowering the likes of which had rarely been seen. However, its incandescent qualities were all but lost on Bathsheba.

"Bath-shua," Vesta coaxed affectionately, using a pet name from her mistress's childhood, "don't miss the spring—here you are, all shut up in your room wasting away to nothing. It seems to me, there's no need to be so sad." Vesta opened the shutters as she scolded. The sunlight and blossom-perfumed air rushed in.

The old servant felt she'd earned the right to speak her mind for she'd been a nurse and do-it-all servant in the house of Eliam, Bathsheba's father, all her years. She had even been born in Gilah into the house of Bathsheba's grandfather, Ahitophel. To Vesta, her "Bath-shua" was more daughter than mistress, and she was more mother than servant.

The woman's voice, crackling with age, grew sharper now as she admonished, "You know Master Uriah will return home as soon as the war ends. But if you stay shut up here, crying day and night, it will make you old and ugly before your time—maybe even before me!"

Vesta's time-worn eyes twinkled momentarily. Bathsheba glanced up from her bed and acknowledged the attempt of humor with a slight smile. The bonds of love had grown thick between them, but at the moment, Bathsheba's spirit of despair overrode all other emotions.

"I'm sorry, Vesta, dear. But I'm tired and very weary of pretending everything is right within me. It just isn't anymore. I know Uriah will return, but to what? To whom? I feel so utterly useless. I've given him no children—no offspring to carry on his name." Bathsheba would have gone on, but Vesta—who had been standing in the doorway with her hands on her ample hips—grew impatient with her mistress; so, she turned away and slowly padded down the hall to the cooking room and the waiting batch of bread dough.

"How could anyone as beautiful and well-married as my little Bath-shua still be unhappy with her lot in life?" Vesta said as she pounded the dough instead of kneading it. *The child has been given everything! She has a face and form even the gods would envy, a faithful husband who would die for her. Yes, she longs for children, but one can live and enjoy life without children if they try,* she reasoned. *After all,* the old woman shook her head rather smugly at the unbaked loaves of bread before her, *I've never had a husband or a baby all these years and I'm just fine.*

Back in her room, Bathsheba wrestled with her feelings and stared idly at the reflected image which peered out at her from the polished bronzed mirror she held.

"You are a mess," she conceded aloud as she began to examine more closely the blotchy and swollen contours of her face. "Everyone says you are so beautiful, but if they could only see you now." Recently she'd begun questioning her attractiveness and today she thought, *I'm almost thirty. Am I beautiful to anyone? Or am I just a withering rose—a brown, dried up leaf. But of what value is outward beauty if inwardly I feel ugly and unsightly?* The thoughts moved uneasily about her soul. *Oh, Uriah, you're always off to war. Do you really need me? I doubt it. And since there are no children in my house, what reasons are there for staying alive? How, without the love of children, can I laugh at the coming of winter in my old age?*

Bathsheba had never before allowed herself to indulge in such selfish and "poor-me" thoughts, but then the disappointments and the pain of her days had never piled up this way before.

Uriah had left her to go to his men without a word, and the unspoken farewell hung like a dark curtain in the corridors of her mind. Even the army runner who brought Uriah's familiar but terse message, "My king needs me, but I shall return to you," was of little comfort to her in her distraught state of mind. And today, to add to it all, the issue of blood which trickled from her loins confirmed and acknowledged the ultimate hurt of her life: she was still barren. Now, with much foreboding, she understood that for another month, and probably the duration of the Ammonite war, there would be no child within her womb to nurture. It was a small but devastating blow to one who wanted a child so much.

"There is no one who understands how I feel, and no one, even if they knew, would care!" Bathsheba cried out miserably as she lay on her bed. Thus she stayed in her room, darkened by the closed shutters, breathing the warm, stale air for several days and nights. Over and over again she wondered what was really the matter with her. *Why can't I get over the disappointment and deal with the dark flashes of my thoughts as I always have done?* she pondered in the darkness.

Finally Bathsheba began to use the solitude to rehash the realities of her life as she perceived them. With an abundance of acrid tears, she found that crying and talking aloud seemed to give some semblance of order to her thinking process, so she stated with precision, "I am angry with the passing of time because it's stealing the childbearing season of my life." True, she had other anxieties over time and what it did to her appearance, but those were incidental fears.

"I am overwhelmed, and am no longer able to adjust to Uriah's long absences—the separations are too painful, too many, and too long." As the wife of a first-rate officer, Bathsheba had always been proud of Uriah's military achievements; and, up to now, she had commended his extreme loyalty to King David. But these feelings were changing. Jealousy, something that had never troubled her before, began breathing down her neck for it seemed Uriah was totally preoccupied with serving his king. Apparently nothing but the army mattered to him, and Bathsheba felt the sting of his obvious rejection. She had no need to ask where his wife fit on the list of her husband's priorities— she knew too well.

But what disturbed Bathsheba's heart the most, in those early days of that glorious spring, was that with the blossoming of plants and trees, the lambing season, and all of nature seemingly giving birth, she could do nothing but mourn for all the children she never had.

Days later, just at sundown, Vesta—who was heartsick over her Bath-shua's forlorn brooding—took matters into her own venerable hands.

"It is enough!" she announced with authority as she marched into Bathsheba's bedroom. She carried a wooden tray with cheese, bread, dried figs, and a silver cup of wine; and, without hesitating a moment, she ordered, "Come!"

Obediently, as she had done in her childhood, Bathsheba got to her feet a bit unsteadily and followed the elderly, white-haired Vesta as she moved stiffly up the narrow steps to the open rooftop. The servant put the tray on a low table and pointed her mistress in the direction of the soft cushions on the floor. She felt proud of herself for she had gotten the mistress released from her self-imposed prison. So, the old woman needed no more words. Warmly she squeezed Bathsheba's shoulder and left the roof. As Vesta made her way back down the steps, the old servant fervently prayed that Jehovah would restore the laughter and the lights in Bath-shua's eyes.

The two-storied home of Uriah, more spacious than most, was situated north of the old mills' section in Jerusalem (or, as it was more commonly known now, the City of David). And just to the rear of their house, a stone's throw away, towered the magnificent palace of King David.

A few years back, King David moved the seat of his royal power from Hebron to Jerusalem; and, when King Hiram of Tyre had heard of the plans, he sent rich gifts of men and material. Carpenters, masons, cedar wood, and other building supplies—all were sent so David could have a home befitting a king. The palace structure turned out to be as enormous as it was opulent.

After Vesta took her leave, Bathsheba left her food tray, and moved from the cushions. Sitting on the low narrow wall edging the roof, she looked up and over at their neighbor's palatial edifice. In the gathering dusk, the palace's pink-hued limestone walls, awning-covered porticos, and rectangular windows which were shuttered with latticed cedar wood, were all impressively elegant. In a small way, viewing the beauty of the building eased the tautness of her soul.

However, a moment later her stomach rumbled (as though she needed a reminder), and Bathsheba realized that it had been days since she had eaten anything of substance. So, giving in to Vesta's tray, she sighed and settled down on the cushions under the canopied back side of the roof and began to pick at her food.

It tasted better than she had supposed it would; and she was just finishing off the figs, thinking how delicious they had been when Vesta returned. It was then both women heard the music.

The sounds were unmistakably the dulcet tones from a small, stringed harp. The song, with its haunting minor refrain, floated down over the neighboring roofs, and its tantalizing melodic lines added a sweetness to the already fragrant spring evening winds.

"But no one plays the lyre like King David!" Bathsheba whispered to Vesta. "Who lives at the palace now that has the king's musicianship and expertise?" she asked.

"Can't you tell?" the old woman squinted upward towards the palace.

"No. It's too dark. I can't see the person, but surely it *isn't* King David," she stated. *For the king to be home when his men are at war is unthinkable,* Bathsheba thought incredulously. *Kings always go into battle. Our David leads his men. It's David who is the first to take up the cudgel, the sword, or any other weapon for the fight. And the sight of their king, his royal presence, in the midst of the battlefield, is what makes most soldiers willingly, without a second thought, lay down their lives.*

"Of course it's King David," Vesta said. But even as she spoke she realized that Bathsheba, because she had kept herself away in her room, had not heard that the king had remained in Jerusalem.

"No!" Bathsheba protested. "He would never desert his men during a war. He wouldn't stay here, enjoying the safety and the comforts of his own home, if his men were out in the battlefields. It's not like him! Our king is a fearless warrior, and he's with General Joab, Uriah, and the troops at Rabbah!"

"Our king," Vesta said testily, "is a lazy warrior, and *this* time he stayed home."

"That's a lie!" Bathsheba's voice pierced the darkness.

"Listen to the music, my child." Vesta touched the younger woman's face. "Your ears will not lie to you." Vesta started for the stairway, but turned back to add, "One of the most reliable palace servant girls told me herself that the king did *not* go with his army this time. He roams about the palace halls, in a very bad mood, and everyone tries to stay out of his way. Even his seven wives and only-Jehovah-knows-how-many concubines have not eased the man's troubled mind."

Bathsheba was stunned. She could not believe this of David. Well she knew that Vesta, for her own reasons, had no love for the king; but her word was quite reliable when it came to the inner workings of the royal household. *However, staying home from a war? How could this be true?*

"My old dear," Bathsheba softened her voice, "you are probably the only woman in all of Israel who has not fallen in love with King David or succumbed to at least one of his many charms."

"I don't know about that." Vesta side-stepped the issue a bit gruffly. "But, I'll tell you, Mistress, sending an army out to war without their king is an evil thing. Mark my words, the man is up to no good, and it's no wonder he prowls about like a restless lion." And with this pronouncement, Vesta retreated downstairs.

Bathsheba moved out from under the canopy and stood by the roof's edge. The music was indeed beautiful, and undeniably the artistry of King David. He was proficient on many instruments, a musician of first-rate talents. Several times she and Uriah had been invited to the royal court and had listened raptly to the king's singing and his instrumental music. But as a harpist, David's talent was greater than any other musician in all of Israel.

As she listened to him, Bathsheba said unto the dark sky, "So, I am not the only one who questions life and doubts its promises. Our great and famous King David is similarly afflicted. Is it possible you suffer from the same dubious thoughts as I? What is it that troubles your spirit so greatly that you do the unheard of thing . . . you send your men away to war while you stay home?"

Long after the music ended and she had returned to her room, Bathsheba lay on her bed contemplating the king's refusal to be with his troops.

Don't you know that as Israel's king you are beloved and respected? Hasn't it occurred to you that when the Hebrew women come out to meet you after a victory—lining the country roads and city streets to sing and dance in honor and praise of you—that it is a true reflection of all our devotion? Is it not enough that Jehovah Himself has heaped blessings and victories upon your head? Have you forgotten that the rewards and plunder from all the wars have added to Israel's treasury and that you have amassed riches beyond all of our ability to comprehend? How could you feel anything less than victorious? You are the supreme ruler.

Then, startled by her own thoughts, Bathsheba sat up in bed and said out loud, "Or, are you troubled, my king, because you are like me? While we have so much, yet we yearn for something or someone more? What is it you long for? Is it something your vast power and your affluent kingdom cannot purchase at any cost?"

With me it's the all-consuming need to have a child, she poignantly remembered. *But I wonder, what could a highly prosperous king lack? What small void within you eludes the filling, my lord?*

Sensing rather by insight than by fact that she had inadvertently stumbled onto the whys of the king's conduct, she pursued her line of reasoning throughout the long night.

David is at the absolute height of his reign. Only the second of Israel's kings, yet he has conquered every enemy; and God has crowned his efforts with unbelievable success. With a mixture of pride and awe, Bathsheba mentally ticked off his accomplishments.

Is our glorious king now wondering what new worlds are left to conquer? Is he looking for new and more difficult challenges? Are these the reasons for his restless wandering through the palace corridors? My lord, have you seen all your dreams, one by one, fulfilled; or, is there some illusive dream, shimmering like a star on the outer edges of your horizon? Are you fresh out of conquests? Bored? Feeling rejected by someone? Lonely?

Or, David, my king, is it simply that you need a friend to believe in you—not for what you do, but for who you are? Do you long for someone to play the harp for you? Someone to play and soothe your heart much like you did for King Saul, when you were just a boy? Or are you still grieving in the secret chambers of your heart over the death of Jonathan, your friend?

"That's it . . . isn't it?" Bathsheba cried aloud. "The hideous price of leadership is the loneliness—the absence of one human being whom you can trust and with whom you can just be yourself!

"You have no one now," she said pragmatically. "Not even the excellent wines from your vast cellars can quench your painful thirst. And I suspect that none of your wives or even the women of your harem are really caring for the sufferings of your soul, are they?"

Once, at a royal function in the palace, Bathsheba had been within arm's length of Abigail and had known, without any reservation, that she was a woman of beauty and wisdom. Now Bathsheba wondered, *my king, do you not speak and bare your hidden soul even to the wise and lovely Abigail?*

Probably not, she answered herself. *Otherwise it wouldn't have been necessary to stay at home, to attempt to console yourself with your harp. You need a friend.*

"Oh, David, David . . ." Bathsheba whispered in genuine concern during the early morning hours. She had been astounded to find that she cared, really *cared* for the king. She was not awe-struck over his position, or the wealth and power which came with the throne, but by the man . . . the man himself.

For the next few nights, Bathsheba quietly stole up to the roof without Vesta and the servants knowing, in the hopes of catching sight of David. It was the best she could do. To seek an audience with a ruling monarch could be arranged, but it was extremely difficult. One had to be officially summoned for an audience with a king. But she began to be obsessed with the desire to *be* with David. She wanted to listen to him, to talk to him, and, mostly, to be a friend to him. *The friend,* she felt, *he longs for.*

Within a few days, nature innocently aided and abetted Bathsheba's desires. The pleasant spring days turned unseasonably and unbearably hot. No cooling breezes came at dusk, and even the dry fiery winds off the desert disappeared. The City of David sweltered in the oppressive heat for six long days.

In order to get some relief from the furnacelike heat and the toll it exacted from everyone's spirit and physical strength, the citizens of Jerusalem tried many things. Some arose unusually early to accomplish the day's chores. Others chose to break their normal routine with an extended meal at noonday or with a shortened workday. Bathsheba, as her daily refuge, took to the roof late in the afternoon. She waited until the major heat of the sun had passed over, and then she took her daily bath up on the roof and let the last remaining rays of the sun dry her body and the fine-spun tresses of her hair.

However, one of those afternoons there was no escape from the sweltering weather, even up on the rooftop. She had bathed and drenched herself with water, yet it had given no relief. That evening the heat only became more intense and Bathsheba, like everyone else, was unable to sleep. So, after a couple of hours of turning and tossing on her damp bed, she finally decided to leave her room and try the roof, in the hope of finding a breath of air and possibly getting some rest.

Unfortunately the rooftop was just as hot as her room. But the moon was full, and she could see the city around her glowing in the pallid light. Bathsheba marveled at the serene beauty of the night for a brief moment, but, once again she was almost overcome with the stifling heat. Noticing that there was still some water left in the jar from her afternoon bath, she poured it out into her wash basin and unbraided her hair.

After Bathsheba immersed her head in the tepid water, she revived a bit and felt refreshed for the first time in days. Then she poured the remaining basin of water on a thirsty-looking plant in a container close by and sat down on some cloths which had been left to dry on the parapet at the roof's edge.

The City of David, its houses clearly visible by the moonlight, was unusually silent as though no one had the strength to speak or to move about in the burning night. She put her head back and began to idly separate the wet strands of her hair with her fingertips.

As she sat there, her head tilted skyward and water dripping down her bare shoulders, she began to have the strange feeling that someone was watching her. In fact, she was sure she was being watched. Moving only her eyes, Bathsheba scanned the palace windows and balconies and finally searched farther up to the balustraded rooftop. There, clearly outlined in the moon's glow, was a familiar form. The king was looking down, standing quite still, intently observing her. The discovery sent a shiver down her back.

Instead of retreating to the canopied side of the roof, as modesty and her culture would have demanded, Bathsheba stayed where she was; and, with a casual deliberateness, went on with the drying of her hair.

When she looked up again, David had been joined by another man. Bathsheba could not tell if it was Benaiah, commander of the king's bodyguards, or Seriah, David's private secretary; but whoever it was, they had a brief discussion and then David was alone again.

Do you find me beautiful, my king? Bathsheba dearly wished she knew as now *she* watched him.

She had no way of knowing how much the soft, diffused light of the moon had added to the alluring splendor of her glistening wet body. But none of the captivating rhapsody, played out on the rooftop below the king, had escaped his notice or failed to excite and kindle his desires.

He summoned her at once.

When his passion drained from him, David did not leave his bed, as was his custom, dismissing the woman from his royal presence; but stayed still in her embrace. For a long time they lay together—peaceably, lazily, without words—neither one wanting to break the shimmering spell of their pleasure.

Finally, in the dark, hot hush of the night, Bathsheba broke the silence with a gentle question. "David, my lord, tell me of Jonathan. Do you miss him greatly?"

She felt his chest move with the sudden intake of his breath. Overwhelmed with a deluge of unexplainable love for her, David looked at the woman in his arms. He marveled that in a few hours she had captured him and had made him her prisoner—her willing prisoner. And now her words, like a small knife, had laid back the coverings of his soul. He was not offended, only surprised at her perceptive mind. She had, in one sentence, exposed the most painfully raw memory of his life.

"How did you know I still grieve for him?" he whispered, his tone incredulous.

"I just know," she traced his cheekbone with her fingertips and waited quietly for him to respond. And respond he did, for after that, David found himself opening the secret chambers of his heart not only about Jonathan, but about his life and feelings as well. He relived the memories of his extreme loneliness as a shepherd boy. He recalled how desperately he'd tried to be friends with his brothers and how it had never happened. And with lumps of unshed tears collecting in his throat, he pulled Bathsheba closer and spoke of Jonathan, who had become the brother he'd never had. As he traced, for her, his and Jonathan's friendship, the chilling reality of Jonathan's death gripped his heart. And it squeezed so hard that the magnificent king began to weep. Bathsheba listened and watched as throbbing sobs convulsed his body and tears ran down his face to mingle with hers.

Then, when he had quieted, Bathsheba said, "We were told that when King Saul and Jonathan were buried, you sang over their graves." David nodded silently. "You remember the song—could you sing it for me . . . now?"

Without a word, David left his bed, crossed the room to the basin of water, and washed and dried his face. When he got back into bed beside Bathsheba, he held her gently in his arms and softly began to sing.

O Israel, your pride and joy lies
    dead upon the hills;
Mighty heroes have fallen.
    Don't tell the Philistines, lest they rejoice.
Hide it from the cities of Gath and Ashkelon,
Lest the heathen nations laugh in triumph.
    O Mount Gilboa,
Let there be no dew nor rain upon you,
Let no crops of grain grow on your slopes.
For there the mighty Saul has died;
He is God's appointed king no more.
    Both Saul and Jonathan slew their strongest foes,
And did not return from battle empty-handed.
    How much they were loved, how wonderful they were—
Both Saul and Jonathan!
They were together in life and in death.

They were swifter than eagles, stronger than lions.
But now, O women of Israel, weep for Saul;
He enriched you
With fine clothing and golden ornaments.
These mighty heroes have fallen in the midst of the battle.
Jonathan is slain upon the hills.
How I weep for you, my brother Jonathan;
How much I loved you!
And your love for me was deeper
Than the love of women!
The mighty ones have fallen,
Stripped of their weapons, and dead.

Softly he repeated, "The mighty ones have fallen, stripped of their weapons, and dead." And Bathsheba cried with the poignant beauty of the song, the tribute, the voice, and the man who sang.

It was then that David, Israel's much-loved king, realized that he had found in one exquisite woman all the love he'd ever yearned for.

When David had looked upon the sensually beautiful Bathsheba, from his royal perch, he had been consumed by the magnitude of his desires. He had felt nothing but his biting, scarlet-colored lust. However, sometime after his first moonlit glimpse of her, sometime in the hours which followed, before the morning sun had traced latticed window patterns across his bedroom floor, David's fiery lust had burnished down to a soft, golden-hued love. There could be no other word for it. It was love. Love, not lust, stunned his senses, surprising him into the realization that, though he had seven wives and many other women in his harem, it was only one—this one—that he wanted to hold forever.

Because his vast experiences with wives and concubines was varied and frequent enough, Israel's second king knew his encounter with the wife of Uriah was neither routinely repetitious nor wildly exotic. It was of a different mode:

intense and deliberate. He gave himself to her as one who had searched in vain until suddenly, without warning, he had discovered and found her. It was as though, when their bodies interlaced, they ceased to be two people.

Bathsheba seemed to fill up the hollow places in his heart. She drew him out by her well-phrased questions and sensitive comments. He bared his soul with her, revealing his doubts and his most painful mistakes. And David also shared his most secret and most noble hope—that one day a son of his would have the mind and the heart to build the opulent temple to God that he already envisioned.

As the early morning light filtered through the window, David was once again overwhelmed by Bathsheba's beauty. Her skin, the color of warm cream, was flawless, and her brown hair, cascading in ripples across the pillows, glowed with red highlights as it trapped the morning sun. As David studied each feature of her face, he determined never to let her go. Some way he'd take her as his wife; he'd make her his queen.

Immersed in his new-found love, and with his awareness of her beauty and spirit, David wanted to give Bathsheba something—anything, everything. He murmured, "You know that when you are with a king it is customary to ask a favor of him. So, what is it I can give you, Bathsheba?" Her eyes shone with the radiance of the morning, but she gave no answer.

David kissed her neck. "Come, tell me," he urged. "My kingdom is yours. Ask what you wish. What is your greatest desire?"

She was studying the boyish handsomeness of his face now, and without taking her eyes off him she finally answered softly, "A child."

"A child?" David drew back, surprised at her words but even more surprised at his own thoughts, for the idea of a son by this woman appealed to him. But . . .

Then, leaning forward, he brushed a stray curl off her

forehead and smiled. "That's what you want?" he asked. "Tell me about it."

"Tell you about what, my lord?" she asked, puzzled.

"Tell me about the wanting of a child."

No one had ever asked, she thought. *No one had ever ventured to ask, cared to ask, or troubled themselves to ask.* Bathsheba found it her turn to be overwhelmed, and indeed she was. A dam of love broke over her soul for this gentle yet powerful warrior king; and, without a moment's hesitation, she unlocked one door after another within her.

David's prodding, careful and sensitive, freed her soul to push past the barriers of her own self-doubts and troubling fears. Whereas formerly she had felt like a brown, dried-up leaf, about to be crumpled up and blown away by the winds of time, now she felt revived, young, supple, and fresh as the tenderest of green, spring leaves. She'd never known such freedom or such ecstasy.

A little more than a month later, Bathsheba sent the king of Israel the single most precious communiqué of her entire life: "I am with child." And the real holocaust of their lives began.

Some said a madness, reminiscent of their former King Saul, took possession of David's soul. For in truth, while he was joyous that he had given Bathsheba a child, the excruciating guilt of his liaison with her and the frantic need to keep this a secret began a series of breathtaking and debilitating effects on him. It did, indeed, produce a cunning madness. But, in order to give legitimacy to the child and to screen himself from exposure, although the night of passion was well known throughout the palace, David resorted to one of the most wicked strategies of his reign.

First he brought Uriah home from the war, gave him presents, and all but ordered him to sleep with Bathsheba. But David's attempt at a cover-up failed because the "loyal soldier" inside Uriah could not, in good conscience, eat and sleep in the comfort of his home while the army and the soldiers under his command camped in open fields.

Frustrated, but still hoping to have Uriah cohabit with Bathsheba so the child would appear to be his, David invited the warrior for dinner. He was generous with the wines and got Uriah drunk, expecting that he would go home to sleep in his own bed that night.

However, Uriah stamped out the king's last hopes by staying away, once more, from his wife. He spent the night, instead, just inside the palace gates. So strong was his loyalty to King David and Israel's cause that, even when inebriated, his innermost fiber would not allow the dedicated soldier in him the luxury of lowering his professional standards. In so doing, Uriah brought about his own death. It was, in fact, only a matter of hours before King David's most heinous act was accomplished.

Ironically, Uriah unknowingly carried back to his commanding general, Joab, the actual orders for his own death sentence.

Later, much later, it was written that God, while He knew David was a sinner, did not end the line of David's royal descendants. And boldly the writers declared, "For David had obeyed God during his entire life *except* for the affair concerning Uriah the Hittite."

As the men of Jabesh-Gilead had fasted and mourned for seven days, after cremating the remains of Saul and his sons, so did Bathsheba mourn for her husband Uriah. But when the seven days of mourning ended, David sent for her; and, with Vesta and two other servant girls, the newly widowed woman moved into the palace. She became one of David's wives, and after her full term was completed she gave birth to a son.

Neither David nor Bathsheba would have ever suspected the depth and breadth of God's displeasure over the actions of their lives had it not been for the intrusion of the incredibly courageous prophet Nathan.

Taking his very life in his hands, Nathan came to the

palace and became God's fearless chastising rod of truth. His words were verbal blows straight from the hand of God. Truth stripped the king of all secret pretenses, and when Nathan had finished, David stood naked and humbled without the masks of his royal identity.

David's confession was instantaneous. "I have sinned against God," he cried in anguish. The prophet nodded his white head solemnly and assured the broken king that he'd been forgiven, but then stunned David with his words: "While the Lord has forgiven you, and you won't die for this sin, you have given great opportunity to the enemies of the Lord to despise and blaspheme Him, so your child shall die." And having nothing more the Lord wanted him to say, Nathan left the palace.

Immediately David summoned her, and a bewildered, trembling Bathsheba stood before him. In her arms she held their limp and feverish son. He had been fine this morning, but suddenly everything was wrong.

"What happened?" she whispered frantically. "Something afflicts our baby. Look at him, my lord."

David turned his face away from her. For all his ability with writing prose and the lyrics for his songs, he could find no way to tell her what he knew for certain was happening.

Bathsheba sank to her knees on the floor before David's throne, and with glazed eyes she held her son—rocking him back and forth—oblivious to all who stood by and watched.

The young infant, almost three months old now, was the most integral part of her joy, the overwhelming gladness of her existence; and his little countenance, so like his father's filled Bathsheba's heart almost to the bursting point with love. Now his face was flushed, and it was too great an effort for him to keep his eyes open. She continued to rock him. "You've fulfilled my dreams, little one." she crooned into the soft, golden halo of hair around his head.

She would have stayed with her baby locked in her

embrace forever had he let her, but gently David took his son and helped Bathsheba into his private chambers. In seven days, despite David's pleading and fasting for God to spare his son, their son died. And what had been conceived in the ecstasy of love was ended in the anguish of grief.

David and Bathsheba mourned not only for their beautiful baby boy, but for the loss of their right-standing with God.

Months before when Uriah died, Bathsheba had keenly felt the loss. She had truly mourned his passing for he had been a kind man, a loyal soldier, and had never intended her any harm. But her bereavement over the loss of the baby was a different thing altogether. She was overwhelmed by the angry indignation every mother feels whose child dies before she does. Hardest by far was that each morning Bathsheba would wake and momentarily be flooded with joy because she was David's wife and the mother of his child. Happily, she'd reach out to hold and nurse her son, and then truth, like an immense stone, would come crashing down on her with new devastation.

David moved her out of his wives' quarters and settled her into the rooms of his own private chambers. There, night and day, he spoke to the needs of her grief. He sang to her trying to soothe her fragmented spirit. He affirmed his deepening love for her, and eventually did what he wanted most desperately to do—he succeeded in comforting her.

Many months later, when she'd grown stronger, Bathsheba requested an immediate audience with the king. It was as though she could wait no longer, not even until nightfall.

David summoned her as soon as he'd been given the message. Now he was awe-struck as he saw her entering his throne room. Her head was held high, and she walked with a regal precision down the long carpet toward him. As she neared him, the light in her eyes was dazzling, and suddenly he gripped the arms of his throne. He knew! He knew exactly what she had to say, and his heart nearly stopped with the rapture of the moment.

When Bathsheba was directly below his dais, she looked up, and David was smitten anew by her beauty. "God has forgiven us, my lord, for I am with child again." Her words flooded his soul with joy.

They *would* survive. Bathsheba just felt it in her heart. *Together* David and she would endure. She was also confident that the natural laws of sin's consequences would make their survival and endurance a very, very delicate and fragile process.

It was David she worried the most over; for he, being the chosen leader of Israel, was suffering what had to be the heaviest brunt of God's scathing displeasure. And it was the nights which seemed to be the hardest ordeal of all for David to endure.

Sometimes his tossing and restless turnings, his sighs and moanings, stretched on for hours during the night. Several times Bathsheba would gently kiss his shoulder to wake him out of his dreadful dreams; and then, rubbing his back with scented oils, she'd soothe and calm his spirit so that eventually he'd become drowsy and fall asleep. But lately, Bathsheba had awakened on several occasions, moved to lie closer to David, only to discover that he was gone. It always startled her even though she knew she'd see him the next day.

To her joy, their lovemaking had remained a small island of intimate pleasure—as it had been from the very beginning. It was marred only by the fact that, instead of lying together and talking after their bodies found their sweet satisfactions, now David grew quiet, almost sullen. It seemed that no matter how she cajoled or coaxed him, he would not respond or share his heart as he had once done so freely.

Tonight David, wide awake, was lying on his back with both hands clasped behind his head, staring at the elaborate paintings on the ceiling above the bed. Bathsheba raised up on one elbow and studied the magnificently handsome face of her husband. But what she saw alarmed her dreadfully. There was a gray, haggard look to his face which gave his forehead and cheeks a waxen, deathlike pallor. To her, he was still the most beautiful man in the world—perfect in face, form, and heart. But, looking at him now, the reality of his suffering was obvious, and she choked back the tears.

"What are you thinking, Bathsheba?" His question startled her, for he'd spoken without turning his face toward her.

"That I love you more dearly than I ever thought could be possible."

In the flickering light of the oil lamp, she saw her husband's tender smile and heard, "I love you, too. But you didn't answer my question. What were you thinking, just then?"

Bathsheba put her head on his chest and responded, "I was thinking about your looks."

"My looks?" David laughed.

"Yes, to me, you have always looked like a proud, strong eagle, soaring to unbelievable heights. But now, since the problems I have brought to your life . . . since Uriah's

death . . . since Nathan . . . and since our baby's . . ."
She stopped, sat up on the bed beside him, took his face
in her hands, and said with sadness, "You are still an eagle,
but now you lie with both wings maimed, your feet broken
and bruised. You must be in anguish, wondering if you'll
ever soar and fly to those rapturous heights again."

For a second David said nothing. Then, in one quick
movement, he brought Bathsheba to him, nearly crushing
her in his arms. He cried out fiercely, "Oh, my God . . .
my God," and a storm of weeping broke from within him.

What seemed like hours later, when he had calmed down
and there were no more tears left to shed, Bathsheba rose
from their bed, crossed the room, and from a small tray
poured him a goblet of wine. He accepted her hospitality
and drank slowly and gratefully.

"Now, it's my turn," she said, as she slipped back to
bed and into the encirclement of his arm.

"For what?" he asked.

"To ask you what you were thinking of—not only tonight, but all those other nights when you kept your
thoughts locked away inside you."

David hesitated. His chest moved with a massive sigh;
but this woman, so perceptive, so lovely, had captured his
heart, and he could not shut her out.

It was true she had been with him through the holocaust.
From the first moment of their lovemaking, she had known
all and seen all. To David, it seemed that the ecstasy of
taking her to his bed, and all the hideous agony of the
events which followed, rested on his shoulders alone.

Now, willing to risk the vulnerability that total honesty
requires, David unburdened his soul; and, in doing so,
Bathsheba saw the full enormity of his fragmented spirit.

"Night after night, I go over Samuel's words and teaching," he said. "How I wish he were here today. Bathsheba,
that old giant of the faith laid down the principles a man
of God should live by. Over and over, even when I was
just a lad fresh out of my father's sheep pastures, Samuel

drilled into me the duties and responsibilities that I would
have as king of Israel. He used Moses' words, and I thought
I'd never forget or violate them . . . but I have. I have."
He shook his head remorsefully.

"What were Moses' instructions about Israel's king?"
Bathsheba inquired.

David thought for a moment, then began to recite the
statutes: "When you arrive in the land your God will give
you, and have conquered it, and begin to think, 'We ought
to have a king like the other nations around us,' be sure
that you select as king the man the Lord your God shall
choose. The requirements are that he must be an Israelite,
not a foreigner. Be sure that he doesn't build up a large
stable of horses for himself, nor send his men to Egypt to
raise horses for him there, for the Lord has told you, 'Never
return to Egypt again.' " Here David gave a low chuckle.
"Moses had firsthand knowledge and experience with Egyptians, so he probably gave the advice to never go back to
Egypt with a great shout of conviction!"

The brief sparkle of mirth left David's eyes and, looking
forlorn again, he continued. "The laws that were set down
for Israel's leader also said that the king must not have
too many wives, lest his heart be turned away from the
Lord—and that he should not be excessively rich." David
broke away from Bathsheba's embrace, and sitting up, he
pushed the pillows up against the bed's ornate ivory and
gold headboard.

"My love," he said as he pulled on his beard, "I am
now that king. I'm a Hebrew. My large stable of horses
is not for myself, but for my army. I have not sent men
to breed and raise horses in Egypt, nor have I ever gone
there, but I have violated some of the principles—I *have*
too many wives, and I *am,* personally, excessively rich."

"But surely, as king, you have kept other laws?"
Bathsheba took one of his large hands in hers and caressed
it lightly. "I've seen you reading the laws from the book

kept by the Levite priests. You never miss a day. Isn't that mandatory also for a king?"

The monarch was pleased with his wife's mental deductions, for he'd never formally told her what he was reading or exactly why.

"Yes, in fact, Samuel said that regular reading of God's laws would prevent a king from feeling that he was better than his fellow citizens. Also, continually absorbing the laws would prevent a king from ever turning away from those very laws in the slightest respect. Furthermore, he said that daily reading of the priests' book would ensure a king of having a long, good reign. Samuel stressed the importance of making God's laws my own by assuring me, in a fatherly way, that if I obeyed these laws my sons would then follow me to the throne of Israel.

Together they lay quietly, with the preponderance of what David had recalled weighing heavily between them. The moments passed in silence as dawn approached and Bathsheba stirred uneasily as David left their bed and pulled a finely woven linen tunic over his head and body.

"It's not morning yet, my lord. Where are you going?"

"I'll be back soon. I promise," he said, evading the issue.

Bathsheba, feeling euphoric for having just experienced their first sharing time in so long, bounded out of bed. And wrapping herself in a purple-hued mantle, she announced, "I'm going with you."

David shrugged his shoulders, and taking a small oil lamp with him, left their bedchamber to go through several adjacent rooms into his private wing of the palace. When he reached the right room, he opened a beautifully carved cedar door and ushered her in.

The room was a large square one with a high ceiling and three long, narrow windows on the outside wall. David opened all the shutters, and Bathsheba caught her breath in surprise. "So this is where you write!" she exclaimed. The predawn light from the windows and the light from the oil lamps combined to reveal a richly carpeted room devoid of all furnishings other than a long, low table and some soft, thick seating cushions. On the table lay papyrus and parchment papers, pots of lampblack ink, which had been made liquid with gallnut juice, and two wide-necked alabaster jars filled with reed pens and various writing points.

But everywhere Bathsheba looked there were scrolls. Some were rolled and stacked in the open bins lining an inner wall. Others were unrolled, held open by gold paper weights; and, spread out like that, they made a carpet of their own on the floor.

David was standing by a window, just watching her, as she took in every detail of his secluded hideaway.

"Is this where you come when you leave me in the middle of the night?" she asked, knowing the answer even as she spoke. David nodded affirmatively.

Bathsheba moved through the writings, careful not to step on any, and putting her arms around David's neck, she urged, "Read them to me. Please."

"No, I can't." He took her arms away from his neck. "No one has read these words. I'm not . . . I'm not sure I ever want anyone to see these writings, or to hear my thoughts." He turned away from her and stared vacantly out the window.

Bathsheba encircled his waist with her arms and, laying her face on the broad expanse at the back of his shoulders, she whispered, "My lord, the *only* thing that can really hurt and damn our souls is our squelching of the pent-up feelings and confessions of our hearts. But you have poured this out to God. Surely He will hear your cry. That's why you find such solace here in your writing, and why you seek out this room so frequently. Here you are free to be yourself before God. Here you are free to release the evil memories which eat away at you."

Gently she pulled him around till he faced her and said, "My king and my husband, read to me. Read me everything you have written; for, like you, I need to be released from the terrible anguish of my stricken conscience. Whatever it is you have written here, I am a part of it all. Remember? 'I am you, you are me, and we are one.' "

Tears began to stream down the flawless beauty of her face; and as the first pink twinge of dawn streaked the sky, David settled Bathsheba gently down upon the cushions. Then, selecting a scroll from the wall bin, he sat down beside her and began,

O loving and kind God, have mercy. Have pity upon me and take away the awful stain of my transgressions. Oh, wash me, cleanse me from this guilt. Let me be pure again. For I admit my shameful deed—it haunts me day and night. It is against you and you alone I sinned, and did this terrible thing. You saw it all, and your sentence against me is just. But I was born a sinner, yes, from the moment my mother conceived me. You deserve honesty from the heart; yes, utter sincerity and truthfulness. Oh, give me this wisdom.

Sprinkle me with the cleansing blood and I shall be clean again. Wash me and I shall be whiter than snow. And after you have punished me, give me back my joy again. Don't keep looking at my sins—erase them from your sight. Create in me a new, clean heart, O God, filled with clean thoughts and right desires. Don't toss me aside, banished forever from your presence. Don't take your Holy Spirit from me. Restore to me again the joy of your salvation, and make me willing to obey you. Then I will teach your ways to other sinners, and they—guilty like me—will repent and return to you. Don't sentence me to death. O my God, you alone can rescue me. Then I will sing of your forgiveness, for my lips will be unsealed—oh, how I will praise you.

You don't want penance; if you did, how gladly I would do it! You aren't interested in offerings burned before you on the altar. It is a broken spirit you want—remorse and penitence. A broken and a contrite heart, O God, you will not ignore.

And Lord, don't punish Israel for my sins—help your people and protect Jerusalem.

And when my heart is right, then you will rejoice in the good that I do and in the bullocks I bring to sacrifice upon your altar.

Bathsheba had wept all through David's reading. The intent of the message had penetrated her soul, and she understood *fully* not only the words, but the magnitude of his writing. As David read, the presence of the Lord of Lords had filled the room, and forgiveness had washed over Bathsheba like the rush of a never-ending mountain stream. It was as though they had been allowed the priestly privilege of going into the Holy of Holies before the ark, and there had had a face-to-face encounter with God.

Looking once again at David, Bathsheba realized that something strange and wonderful was happening. It was written on his face. "David," she cried, "what is this I feel? Is it forgiveness?"

He didn't answer. He was silently rereading his own words, and a look of surprised joy was spreading over his countenance. He knew Nathan had told him he was forgiven, but up to this point David's own acceptance had been nigh unto impossible. He had written and signed his confession to the Lord almost a week ago. He had not reread it until tonight, at Bathsheba's request. God had heard his prayer and, indeed, had answered it—he was beginning now to feel God's forgiveness.

David looked up at Bathsheba as he put the scroll aside. "Yes," he said, "it's forgiveness." He pulled her close, and holding her tightly in his arms, he began to pray to the God he loved and served. In a deep resonant voice, he said with great tenderness,

What happiness for those whose guilt has been forgiven! What joys when sins are covered over! What relief for those who have confessed their sins and God has cleared their record.

There was a time when I wouldn't admit what a sinner I was. But my dishonesty made me miserable and filled my days with frustration. All day and all night your hand was heavy on me. My strength evaporated like water on a sunny day until I finally admitted all my sins to you and stopped trying to hide them. I said to myself, "I will confess them to the Lord." And you forgave me! All my guilt is gone.

I will praise you, Lord, for you have saved me from my enemies. You refuse to let them triumph over me. O Lord my God, I pleaded with you, and you gave me my health again. You brought me back from the brink of the grave, from death itself, and here I am alive!

Oh, I will sing to you, and give thanks to your holy name. Your anger lasts a moment; your favor lasts for life! Weeping may go on all night, but in the morning there is joy.

They stayed wrapped in each other's arms long after he'd finished his prayer. But when they arose and left his writing room, the Hebrew nation had a forgiven king—a stronger king, a wiser king, and an extraordinary queen. For God chose to see Bathsheba also through eyes of mercy and loving forgiveness.

David and Bathsheba would survive the violence and brutality of the next hellish years, but from David's pen would flow the words,

Listen to my prayer, O God; don't hide yourself when I cry to you. Hear me, Lord! Listen to me! For I groan and weep beneath my burden of woe.

My enemies shout against me and threaten me with death. They surround me with terror and plot to kill me. Their fury and hatred rise to engulf me. My heart is in anguish within me. Stark fear overpowers me. Trembling and horror overwhelm me. Oh, for wings like a dove, to fly away and rest! I would fly to the far off deserts and stay there. I would flee to some refuge from all this storm.

Then, in due time, the chastening rod in God's hand would be dropped; and the Lord of all would sweeten the bitter waters Bathsheba and David drank, restoring what He promised—the joy of their salvation.

Bathsheba was to bear David four sons; and God would bless their eldest son, Solomon, by making him his father's successor to the throne.

In his later years, David summed up his life by writing,

> The Lord lifts the fallen and those bent beneath their loads. The eyes of all mankind look up to you for help; you give them their food as they need it. You constantly satisfy the hunger and thirst of every living thing.
>
> The Lord is fair in everything he does, and full of kindness. He is close to all who call on him sincerely. He fulfills the desires of those who reverence and trust him; he hears their cries for help and rescues them. He protects all those who love him, but destroys the wicked.
>
> I will praise the Lord and call on all men everywhere to bless his holy name forever and forever.

In the eyes of God, David and Bathsheba had been forgiven. They had been reconciled to Him. So, He blessed their lives with a peace beyond understanding.

Humbly David wrote, and then read aloud to Bathsheba,

> Lord, many times you have miraculously rescued me, the king you appointed. You have been loving and kind to me and will be to my descendants.
>
> You will give me added years of life, as rich and full as those of many generations, all packed into one. And I shall live before the Lord forever.
>
> Oh, send your loving kindness and truth to guard and watch over me, and I will praise your name continually, fulfilling my vow of praising you each day.

In later years still wrapped in the Lord's mantle of peace, David wrote,

> But as for me, my contentment is not in wealth but in seeing the Lord and knowing all is well between us. And when I

awake in heaven, I will be fully satisfied, for I will see Him face to face.

Centuries later, King David would be remembered as "the man after God's own heart." His queen, Bathsheba, would be granted the singular privilege of being named in the direct lineage of Christ, the true Messiah.

ABOUT THE AUTHOR

Joyce Landorf Heatherley is known nationwide as a uniquely gifted communicator, able to convey biblical principles with
relevance, humor, compassion, and gentle conviction– in ways
that speak to the needs of men and women from all back-
grounds. A best-selling author of both fiction and non-fiction,
her 24 books include: MY BLUE BLANKET, THE INHERI-
TANCE, BALCONY PEOPLE, SILENT SEPTEMBER, MON-
DAY THRU SATURDAY, FRAGILE TIMES, IRREGULAR
PEOPLE, HE BEGAN WITH EVE, CHANGEPOINTS,
UNWORLD PEOPLE, MOURNING SONG, JOSEPH, I CAME
TO LOVE YOU LATE, FRAGRANCE OF BEAUTY, RICHEST
LADY IN TOWN, and her latest title, SPECIAL WORDS,
Notes For When You Don't Know What To Say.

Joyce is also a popular speaker and conference leader.
Recordings of her most requested talks, including BALCONY
PEOPLE, IRREGULAR PEOPLE, MY BLUE BLANKET, and
THE INHERITANCE are available on audio cassette, as are
video tapes of CHANGEPOINTS, IRREGULAR PEOPLE, and
THE INHERITANCE. Her HIS STUBBORN LOVE film series,
based on her nationally acclaimed seminars of the same name,
was the recipient of the president's award from the Christian
Film Distributors Association.

Speaking engagement requests or inquiries concerning
Joyce Landorf Heatherley books, tapes, and music may be
directed to:

1-800-777-7949

Visit our web site at:
www.balconypublishing.com